LORD,

ONLY YOU CAN
CHANGE ME

— B O O K S   B Y   K A Y   A R T H U R —

Lord, Heal My Hurts
Lord, I Want to Know You
Lord, Is It Warfare? Teach Me to Stand
Lord, Where Are You When Bad Things Happen?
Lord, I'm Torn Between Two Masters
Lord, I Need Grace to Make It Today
Lord, Teach Me to Pray in 28 Days
God, Are You There? Do You Care? Do You Know About Me?
How to Study Your Bible Precept upon Precept
The International Inductive Study Series
Beloved: From God's Heart to Yours
His Imprint, My Expression
To Know Him by Name
As Silver Refined
Our Covenant God
Search My Heart, O God
A Sanctuary for Your Soul
My Savior, My Friend
A Moment with God
With an Everlasting Love
Marriage Without Regrets
Discover 4 Yourself Inductive Bible Studies for Kids

LORD,

ONLY YOU CAN CHANGE ME

A DEVOTIONAL STUDY *on* GROWING

IN CHARACTER *from the* BEATITUDES

KAY

ARTHUR

WATERBROOK
PRESS

LORD, ONLY YOU CAN CHANGE ME
PUBLISHED BY WATERBROOK PRESS
12265 Oracle Boulevard, Suite 200
Colorado Springs, Colorado 80921

Portions of this study were previously included in the book *Lord, How Can I Ever Be Righteous?*

ISBN 978-1-57856-436-1
    (previously 0-88070-878-6)

Published in the United States by WaterBrook Multnomah, an imprint of the Crown Publishing Group, a division of Random House Inc., New York.

Library of Congress Cataloging-in-Publication Data

Arthur, Kay, 1933-
    Lord, only you can change me : a devotional study on growing in character from the Beatitudes / Kay Arthur.—[Rev. ed.].
        p. cm.
    Includes bibliographical references.
    ISBN 1-57856-436-0
        1. Sermon on the mount—Study and teaching. 2. Sermon on the mount—Criticism, interpretation, etc. 3. Christian life—Study and teaching. I. Title.

BT380.2 .A79 2001
241.5'3—dc21

                                                          00-068622

Printed in the United States of America
2011

20 19 18 17 16 15 14 13 12

CONTENTS

Introduction vii

Chapter One   Getting Beyond Our Masks 1

Chapter Two   Where True Happiness Begins 19

Chapter Three   Do You Weep over Sin? 45

Chapter Four   Meekness in the Presence of Sovereignty 77

Chapter Five   Meekness: Is It Weakness or Strength? 105

Chapter Six   Hungering and Thirsting for Righteousness 135

Chapter Seven   How Can I Be Merciful…Pure? 163

Chapter Eight   Peacemakers…but Persecuted 191

Chapter Nine   Salt, Light, and You 221

The Sermon on the Mount 247

Study Resources 257

Notes 271

INTRODUCTION

You stand and gaze in the mirror, evaluating what you see—the way you will appear before others on the outside. But what about the inside—the character that counts, that enhances what others see and never belies the appearance you give when you are "on display"? What are you like, Beloved, in the inner man? Is it any different from what you once were? Is there a growing, a changing into His image? Is your character being transformed more and more into His likeness? Are you distinguished from those you work with in the world, as well as from those who call Him, "Lord, Lord" but really don't do the things He tells them to do?

This is a devotional study on character—the character that belongs to those who genuinely belong to God. It will reveal what godly character looks like for you in the home and in the marketplace...in fact, wherever you are. Among many other things, it's about humility (meekness) and mercy and purity—qualities that we're so often deficient in and that we want to grow in until finally we "are perfect even as our Father in heaven is perfect." Built into the definition of this word *perfect* is the idea of maturity, attainment—and that is what we are after in this study, Beloved: growth on the inside that far outshines and outweighs our physical appearance and accomplishments.

You are about to immerse yourself in a study of the Beatitudes to help you mine and explore many spiritual gems that will enrich your life, helping you to prosper spiritually in a way that will delight you and be noticed by others. The water of His Word will bring a growth that will be well worth the discipline of daily study.

This is a study you can do alone—it's used by Christian counselors as part of their counseling. But it is also a study that can be done in groups and even become a ministry for you, Beloved of God, as you desire to reach the hurting of this world and see them healed. If there is that possibility of your using this as a group study in which you would be a facilitator, then read "Guidelines for Group Use" in the "Study Resources" section at the back of this book, where you'll find other valuable tools to enhance this study.

For many, the blessing of this study has been enhanced by the companion video and audio teaching tapes. For more information on these, simply call Precept Ministries International at our toll-free number (1-800-763-8280) and let one of our staff members help you. It would be their pleasure. We also provide training if you would like to develop your skills in handling the Word of God more accurately or in leading others in group studies designed to minister to people of all ages at any level of commitment while respecting the restraints on their time. We're known as "The Inductive Study People: everybody, everywhere, any time, any place, any language, any age. One message: the Bible. One method: inductive." Please don't hesitate to call us.

Finally, let me share my vision—it's the possibility of a new avenue of ministry for you, Beloved of God…

A new beginning—
An avenue of ministry—
A sense of doing something that has eternal value

These are three things I think are so important for you and for me. There's so much to learn, to know, to experience, to do—and we never want to lose sight of that. To do so would be to miss what God has for us. To fall short of the tremendous potential of our lives—a potential that is ours because we are His, because we are children of the Creator of the Universe, indwelt by His divine Spirit and given the mind of Christ. You and I, Beloved, are God's workmanship gifted by the Spirit of God and created in Christ Jesus unto good works that would absolutely stagger our minds if we were to see them before they ever happened.

And what has God put into your hands? What are you holding and reading right now? Is it an accident? A coincidence? No! You are holding a devotional study that first and foremost will be the beginning of a new depth of understanding about growing in godly character.

God is going to speak to you because through this book you are going to come face to face with the living Word of God—the Word that not only discerns the thoughts and intentions of your heart, but becomes the means of throwing His light on the direction your life is taking so you can know with absolute confidence where you are headed. If you listen to what He says—and by that I mean ordering your life accordingly—then there is, in a sense, a new beginning...of understanding, of purpose. A new level of Christlikeness is attained. You will be, as Paul would say, pressing on and attaining that for which Jesus Christ laid hold of you.

Which brings me to my next point—an avenue of ministry. What you have learned, God intends for you to share. I have a vision, and you, Beloved, are part of that vision. Our Lord's commission in Matthew 28 was that we make disciples of all men—that we teach them to observe all that He has commanded us. Acts 1 tells us that when we are saved and receive the Holy Spirit we become His witnesses—yet the question is often, "How?"

Here is the how. This "Lord" book contains truths every human being needs to know and to apply to his or her life. These are precepts for life; through them we will gain understanding and, as the psalmist says, "hate every false way" (Psalm 119:104). We hate it because it is false rather than true, and it is truth that sets us apart, sets us free.

So what is my vision for you, my friend? It is that you go to the Lord in prayer and ask Him to direct you to at least one other person—but preferably at least ten—and that you, along with them, study this book together. You may not be a teacher, but you can be the group's facilitator. You can take the questions you'll find at the end of each chapter and use them to stimulate a discussion among those whom the Lord has brought together in answer to your prayer. These are those who will be part of your crown of rejoicing in the presence of our Lord Jesus Christ. As you watch them learn and grow in the knowledge of God and of His Word, you will experience the humbling joy of knowing that you have been used of God. That what you have done has eternal value. That your life and God-given gifts have not been wasted. That your work will live on—that the grace of God poured out on you was not poured out in vain, for you have labored in the strength of His grace.

So as you facilitate a group using this book, you need to watch for and encourage others in your group to do as you have done—to take what they have learned and impart it to another as you did with them. Think of the multiplication that will happen! Do you realize, Beloved, that this is the way we can reach our neighborhoods, our communities, our nation, and beyond? Think of the transformation that will take place among all those people today who are so interested in "the spiritual" but won't step inside a church. Think—just think!—what is going to happen!

The time is now. The hour is short. Stop and pray right now and ask God what He would have you to do. He will show you, because He is God and because such prayers are in accordance with His will. As you step out and begin, just know that if you will step out in faith, God will give you an avenue of ministry, person by person or group by group, that will not only stagger your mind but absolutely delight your soul.

I cannot wait to hear what God does in and through you, my friend.

GETTING BEYOND OUR MASKS

— D A Y   O N E —

Maybe you've tried and tried and failed and failed. You find yourself thinking, *There is no way I can change! There's no way I can be the man...the woman...the husband...the wife...the parent...the single person...God wants me to be. The task is too great! The odds are insurmountable!*

Or possibly you look around...maybe among your family and friends, maybe among the members of your church, maybe in the body of Christ in general...and shudder because of all the hypocrisy you see. Or maybe you look within and shudder at your own hypocrisy!

You want heaven, but you're getting hell on earth instead. You find yourself clinging to life—sometimes by your fingernails—in the hope that somehow, someday, somewhere life will change and heaven will come to earth. Or perhaps you've already let go in despair. You've resigned yourself to a living hell.

I understand. Truly, I do. I've been there. And you might be surprised to know how many others have been there too.

It really wasn't all that much different in the days when Jesus walked this earth as a human being. He looked around Him and saw men and women and young people trapped in these same situations. They tried and tried—and they failed and failed. Their religion—the storied, richly tapestried faith of their fathers—just wasn't working. Many of those who seemed "in the know" about God and His Word were rank hypocrites.

But rather than condemn these unhappy, harried people, Jesus had deep compassion on them. To His eyes, they looked "distressed and downcast like sheep without a shepherd" (Matthew 9:36). So He went up to a high and beautiful hill beside the Sea of Galilee to set forth the truth from His Father. Overlooking that sea—a sea sometimes peaceful and serene, at other times turbulent and threatening—He sat down with His disciples and told them about the kingdom of heaven. About what belonging to that kingdom would mean in their daily lives. About the changes it would bring. And about the price they would have to pay.

Let's climb that hill too, my friend. It's a breathtaking climb...with a breathtaking view. Let's sit at His feet, high above the restless, changing sea. Let's drink in His words and ponder His perspective. For we too have been "distressed and downcast," and we too need the wisdom and guiding hand of our good Shepherd.

That's your assignment today, Beloved. To sit at His feet and read again His timeless words in Matthew 5–7. Don't mark or underline a single word today. Simply open your heart and read. But before you do...begin with prayer. Tell the Father you want to hear and understand the words of His Son. Tell Him that you long to have the life they can bring. Then, when you've finished your reading, talk to Him again. Talk to Him about what His Son has said. Be honest. Tell Him what you think, what you feel, what you don't understand, what you *want* to understand. Tell Him what you feel is impossible—and why.

Before you get up from your knees, you might tell Him your desire to commit yourself to this nine-week study. Lift up your voice, and cry out to Him, *Lord, only You can change me. Please do. In Jesus' name.*

If you have read through the Word of God, you know how God delights to hear and honor the cry of those who call out to Him with sincere hearts. And He not only hears "saints;" he hears the cry of "sinners" as well. He's heard my cry, and He will hear yours.

I'm going to give you some space to write out your prayer...or perhaps to list those longings of your heart that you'd like to bring before

Him. You don't have to use the space, but you might find it helpful. At the end of this study, you may want to come back and reflect on all He has accomplished in you through these life-transforming weeks.

Now climb that hill! Hear His words. And watch your life begin to change.

— D A Y   T W O —

Real Christian life—the genuine article—is never hypocritical.

Authentic Christian life is something higher, brighter, and infinitely more powerful than pale, phony substitutes.

It will take you from the valley of sin to the mount of blessedness.

It will take you from the depths of destitution to the heights of God's approval.

It will lift you from the instability of building on sand to the security of a foundation on rock.

It is a lifestyle that can endure all the torrential storms of life and remain unshaken.

Where can it be found?

It's all in seed form in Matthew 5, 6, and 7—Jesus' Sermon on the Mount. Today I want us to think about the main theme of this magnificent message. What is its heartbeat? What point is Jesus making?

Two key words that will help us grasp the theme of the Sermon are *righteousness* and *heaven*. Read through the Sermon on the Mount printed at the back of this book and mark every reference you find to *heaven* and *righteousness*, or their synonyms.* You might want to use a blue pen and draw a little cloud shape like this— ◠◠◠◠◠◠ —around each reference to heaven. Whatever design you choose, mark the words in a distinctive way so you can spot them easily. Then choose another color and/or special marking to highlight the words *righteous* and *righteousness* in the text. *Heaven* or *heavenly* is used twenty-one times; *righteous* or *righteousness* appears six times.

When you have finished marking each reference, fill in the appropriate spaces that follow. Note the chapter and verse of each mention of these words, and record what you learn in each passage.

HEAVEN

CHAPTER AND VERSE   WHAT I LEARNED

1. Matthew 5:3   It belongs to the poor in spirit.

2.

3.

4.

5.

6.

* See page 259 for section on marking your Bible.

7.

8.

9.

10.

11.

12.

13.

14.

15.

16.

17.

18.

19.

20.

21.

RIGHTEOUSNESS

CHAPTER AND VERSE   WHAT I LEARNED

1.

2.

3.

4.

5.

What is the theme of the Sermon on the Mount? It is *the righteous lifestyle of those who belong to the kingdom of heaven.* We will look more closely at this theme tomorrow. But before we close…would you allow me one question? What did you learn today that you didn't know before? Write it out.

— D A Y   T H R E E —

From looking at the words *heaven* and *righteousness* you may have noticed that those who will enter the kingdom of heaven fulfill four basic requirements. Let's summarize them.

Those who enter the kingdom of heaven

1. are poor in spirit (5:3);
2. are persecuted for righteousness' sake (5:10);
3. have a righteousness that even surpasses that of the scribes and Pharisees (5:20);
4. obey God's will (7:21).

The bottom line of Jesus' message? Righteousness is an absolute necessity for those who are going to enter the kingdom of heaven! For this reason, I believe the *key verse* for the Sermon on the Mount is Matthew 5:20: "For I say to you, that unless your righteousness surpasses that of the scribes and Pharisees, you shall not enter the kingdom of heaven."

Was it any wonder the multitudes were amazed at Jesus' teaching! A righteousness that *exceeded* the righteousness of the scribes and Pharisees? How could it ever be? These were the great religious leaders of the day. None were more respected than they! How then could such a righteousness be attained by ordinary people—fishermen and carpenters and housewives and passionate young people and children? What could He have meant by those bewildering words?

Understanding the scribes and Pharisees will help you answer these questions and give you deeper insight into Jesus' message in the Sermon on the Mount.

The Old Testament documents the existence of scribes long before the Pharisees entered the stage of history. But they really did not come into prominence until Judah was restored to its land following the Babylonian captivity. The office of scribe came out of the priesthood. Scribes were experts in the Law of Moses whose responsibilities fell into two general categories: preserving the Law and teaching the Law.

The scribes may have been the originators of the synagogues, which came into being as a result of the Babylonian exile. Cut off from the ruined temple of Jerusalem, the Jews created the synagogue as a place where God's people could gather to worship and be instructed in the Law.

By the time of Jesus' birth, the synagogue was one of Judaism's most important institutions. It was in these synagogues that the scribes and Pharisees exercised their considerable authority. They taught the Law, yes. But they taught their own *traditions* and *interpretations* of the Law as well. The man or woman on the street did not own a copy of the Law but depended solely upon the teachings of these religious leaders.

The Pharisees were a religious party which came into being during the four-hundred-year period between the Old and New Testaments. By Jesus' time, they had supreme influence among the people. They believed in the resurrection, angels, spirits, and the coming of the Messiah, but their forte was the Law of God! As a matter of fact, they had reduced God's Law to a code of 365 negative commandments and 250 positive commandments—which included many of their own interpretations of God's Word. They claimed that these expansions came from direct inspiration and were God-given interpretations of the Law. As a result, when the people heard the Word, they heard a distorted version of it. This is why Jesus took the scribes and Pharisees to task so sternly. Their traditions and so-called interpretations often directly contradicted God's intentions. Listen to Jesus' comments.

And He said to them, "Rightly did Isaiah prophesy of you hypocrites, as it is written,

'THIS PEOPLE HONORS ME WITH THEIR LIPS,

BUT THEIR HEART IS FAR AWAY FROM ME.

BUT IN VAIN DO THEY WORSHIP ME,

TEACHING AS DOCTRINES THE PRECEPTS OF MEN.'

"Neglecting the commandment of God, you hold to the tradition of men." He was also saying to them, "You nicely set aside the commandment of God in order to keep your tradition...thus invalidating the word of God by your tradition which you have handed down; and you do many things such as that." (Mark 7:6-9,13)

As a result of the scribes' and Pharisees' interpretation of the Law, sin had become only an external act, rather than a matter of the heart. Something was declared right or wrong because an external condition was absent or present. For instance, if a Jew gave alms to the poor on the Sabbath, he could do so only if the beggar put his hand through the door to receive the alms. If the Jew extended his hand out the door to give alms to the beggar, he was considered to have broken the Sabbath.

Knowing this, you may better understand what Jesus means in Matthew 5 when He says, "You have heard...*but I say to you*" (verses 21-22).They had heard a distortion of the Law from the scribes and Pharisees' teaching in the synagogues, but they didn't know any better because they didn't know God's Word! (No wonder they were so distressed and downcast!)

And isn't that the way it is today? Sometimes I find myself shuddering as I watch "Christian" television. I shudder because I know that thousands upon thousands of untaught Christians are lapping up teachings which are simply not biblical. Yet they don't know better because they don't know God's Word! And they will *never* know it in its purity and authority and true transforming power until they study it for themselves. This is why I have such an intense longing to teach men, women, boys, and girls throughout the world how to study God's Word for themselves—inductively!

Take a moment now, as this day's study ends, and read Mark 7:1-16. Are there any traditions you're holding to which are not truly biblical? What might they be? List them below.

Now ask the Lord to root your life ever deeper by the sure-flowing stream of His eternal Word.

— D A Y   F O U R —

"We live in a time when many who claim to know Christ undermine the Gospel by short-circuiting the radical implications of a life of discipleship as set forth by Jesus the Christ." When I read this statement in Robert Guelich's commentary on the Sermon on the Mount, I thought, *How true that is, and how typical!*

We want heaven, life, eternity! Who doesn't? We hear the good news about eternal life through Jesus Christ. It's free, so we take it, tuck it under our arm, and walk away. We're relieved. No hell now; heaven's our home. Then, since we "have that problem settled," we imagine we can get back to living our lives as we please.

But can we?

Does true Christianity allow us to go back to living *our own lives?*

I would like to switch on a worldwide intercom at this point and shout one loud, resounding NO! You cannot belong to God and live any way you please! True Christianity is discipleship. It's the willingness to turn around, to leave everything, and to let Jesus Christ be all in all. It's the willingness to follow Him wherever He leads and to do whatever He says. True Christianity is a total commitment of oneself to the lordship of Jesus Christ.

Some of you may disagree. That's fine. Just don't stop studying until you see what the Sermon on the Mount has to say—lest you short-circuit the radical implications of the gospel of Jesus Christ.

Read Matthew 7:13-29. Then, from what you have read, answer the questions that follow.

▶ MATTHEW 7:13–29

"Enter by the narrow gate; for the gate is wide, and the way is broad that leads to destruction, and many are those who enter by it. For the gate is small, and the way is narrow that leads to life, and few are those who find it.

"Beware of the false prophets, who come to you in sheep's clothing, but inwardly are ravenous wolves. You will know them by their fruits. Grapes are not gathered from thorn bushes, nor figs from thistles, are they? Even so, every good tree bears good fruit; but the bad tree bears bad fruit. A good tree cannot produce bad fruit, nor can a bad tree produce good fruit. Every tree that does not bear good fruit is cut down and thrown into the fire. So then, you will know them by their fruits. Not everyone who says to Me, 'Lord, Lord,' will enter the kingdom of heaven; but he who does the will of My Father who is in heaven. Many will say to Me on that day, 'Lord, Lord, did we not prophesy in Your name, and in Your name cast out demons, and in Your name perform many miracles?' And then I will declare to them, 'I never knew you; DEPART FROM ME, YOU WHO PRACTICE LAWLESSNESS.'

"Therefore everyone who hears these words of Mine, and acts upon them, may be compared to a wise man, who built his house upon the rock. And the rain descended, and the floods came, and the winds blew, and burst against that house; and yet it did not fall, for it had been founded upon the rock. And everyone who hears these words of Mine, and does not act upon them, will be like a foolish man, who built his house upon the sand. And the rain descended, and the floods came, and the winds blew, and burst against that house; and it fell, and great was its fall."

The result was that when Jesus had finished these words, the multitudes were amazed at His teaching; for He was teaching them as one having authority, and not as their scribes.

1. Describe the way that leads to life.

2. Whose words are you reading in this passage? If you have trouble answering this, look at Matthew 5:1-2 and 7:28-29.

3. According to Jesus, how many are there who find the way to life?

4. Who is going to enter the kingdom of heaven?

5. How do those who are going to heaven respond to Jesus' words?

6. Why do you think the people were amazed at Jesus' teaching in Matthew 5–7?

7. According to what you have just read, do you think a person can live any way he pleases and still go to heaven? Explain your answer.

8. Now, let's get personal. How do *you* live?

− D A Y   F I V E −

Hypocrisy is an age-old problem. And it was as common in Jesus' day as it is today. Jesus used the word frequently, particularly in reference to two groups of people. Take a few minutes and read Matthew 23. As you do, it would be good to color or mark each occurrence of the word *hypocrites* in a distinctive way. Then write in the following space whom Jesus called "hypocrites" and why He called them that.

Hypocrite was the word used for a stage actor. In Greek and Roman theater, actors customarily wore large masks to indicate a particular mood or emotion. No matter how the actor himself might feel, the mask was what everyone saw. A hypocrite, then, is an actor, or one who habitually wears a mask.

From your reading of Matthew 23, why do you think Jesus used the term *hypocrites* to describe the scribes and Pharisees? What were they doing that prompted Him to say what He did? Write out your answer below.

Now, stop and think. Are you a hypocrite in any way? Do you ever find yourself "acting"? Do you ever find yourself slipping on a mask to hide the way you truly feel? Do you speak words that your life does not back up? For instance, when you sing in church "I surrender all…," have you really surrendered all?

When you pray the Lord's Prayer and say, "Lead us not into temptation, but deliver us from evil…," do you really desire to stay away from temptation? When you pray, "Forgive us our trespasses as we forgive those who trespass against us…," are you really willing to forgive others — from the heart—as God has forgiven you? Do you pray at prayer meetings to be seen by others, but not at home when you are alone with God?

What about masks? Do you behave one way at church and another way at home or in your business? Does your attitude toward your mate or your children change when you get out of the car in the church parking lot? Do you slip a smiling-face mask over an angry scowl? Do you pull on an I-really-care-about-you mask when you talk to people, while underneath you really don't care at all?

Do you see what I am saying? It was the *religious* ones whom Jesus called hypocrites. They were the ones who claimed to know God—not the prostitutes, drunks, thieves, liars, and adulterers.

Perhaps at this point you are asking: "Is it possible *not* to be a hypocrite? Doesn't everyone wear a mask now and then? Is it realistic to think my heart can match what I portray on the outside? Can I truly be righteous—inside and out?"

Yes! Yes you can!

You can…or Jesus would have never required it of us. Just remember, what He demands, He supplies. How? By coming to live inside you. By giving you His Holy Spirit who will lead you into all righteousness. Be patient, Beloved. It will all become more clear as this study unfolds in the weeks that follow.

Philip Keller in his autobiography, *Wonder O' the Wind,* wrote:

It was not that we neglected the church, the Word of God, or our daily devotions. We did not. Quite the contrary. Like other millions of modern-day Christians, we went through the regular routine of religious rituals, but they were dry as the dust in my sheep corrals, and just about as barren.

Almost by default I concluded subconsciously that my joy in life could come from the earth and need not come from Christ.

Yet the strange irony of my inner spiritual stagnation was that deep down within my spirit there was an intense hunger to really know God. There persisted an insatiable thirst to commune with Christ. But how?

How? We will see how in the Sermon on the Mount.

The Sermon on the Mount is not a new law or an impossible standard to be reached for but never obtained until the Lord's return. Rather, it is a teaching given by Jesus Himself on the new relationship with Him that is ours through the New Covenant.

The first seven beatitudes (Matthew 5:3-9) show the *character* of those who enter into this relationship. The next two beatitudes (verses 10-12) show the *conflict* that such character brings in a world that does not recognize Jesus' lordship. The remainder of the Sermon (5:13–7:27) shows the *conduct* of those who belong to Jesus. This conduct shows forth the shining presence of God's sovereign rulership in the life of His son or daughter.

So, what is our outline of the Sermon on the Mount?

THE RIGHTEOUS LIFESTYLE OF THOSE
WHO BELONG TO THE KINGDOM OF HEAVEN

Matthew 5:1-2:	Prologue
Matthew 5:3-9:	Their Character
Matthew 5:10-12:	Their Conflict
Matthew 5:13–7:27:	Their Conduct
Matthew 7:28-29:	Epilogue

The Sermon on the Mount is only an impossible lifestyle for those who have not bowed their knees to the King nor yielded up the throne of their hearts to His right to reign as King of kings and Lord of lords!

But if you will but bow—
if you will yield—
the kingdom of heaven,
in all its fullness and joy
will be yours.

It will be yours because God Himself will change you and fit you for the kingdom of heaven. It's the very reason He came among us.

MEMORY VERSE

For I say to you, that unless your righteousness surpasses that of the scribes and Pharisees, you shall not enter the kingdom of heaven.

MATTHEW 5:20

SMALL-GROUP DISCUSSION QUESTIONS

1. As you read the Sermon on the Mount, what made the most significant impression on your mind?
2. What did you learn about righteousness?
3. What did you learn about the kingdom of heaven?
4. According to the Sermon on the Mount, who is going to heaven? What are the four basic requirements of those who will enter the kingdom of heaven?
5. What is the meaning of the word *hypocrite?* How does hypocrisy manifest itself?

6. Is hypocrisy in any form demonstrated in your life? What would others see if they really knew you? Try to be honest, vulnerable, and willing to grow.

7. Is your Christianity working? If not, in which areas are you failing?

8. What, if anything, needs to change in order for your life to become a true mirror image of what is inside?

9. Review the outline of the Sermon on the Mount with its chapter and verse divisions, as given on page 15.

WHERE TRUE
HAPPINESS BEGINS

— D A Y   O N E —

A*ll I want to be is happy!"*
You've heard those words before, haven't you? You've probably *said* those words…if not out loud, then at least in the quiet
corners of your heart.

When was the last time you felt really happy? Can you remember?
Maybe it was one of those *Sound of Music* mornings with the sun spilling
into your bedroom window out of a crystal blue sky. Maybe you felt like
dancing across the mountaintops, twirling and singing. Then again, maybe
you felt like sitting in a sun-splashed corner of your home, sipping coffee
and savoring the morning stillness.

No storms hovered on your horizon.

No dark clouds threatened to rain on your dreams.

Those moments are rare, aren't they? Because all too soon the clouds
of circumstance roll in. All too soon life's storms hide the blue skies and
blot out the sun, making those feelings of happiness seem like a half-
forgotten dream.

Is that the way it will always be in our lives? Will our happiness always
depend on fragile, fickle, changeable circumstances? For most people
those are simply the sad facts of life. They don't really expect much happiness. They don't expect to catch more than a few glimpses of it, glinting
on a faraway horizon.

Happiness of course means different things to different people. Some would describe it as a vague feeling of satisfaction, pleasure, or contentment. Note that I said "feeling." Feelings are usually determined not only by our circumstances but also by our emotions, which can swing like a weather vane in the wind. If our bodies are warm, well fed, and in reasonably good health and our self-image is intact, our "emotion barometer" may show positive readings. But if those variables should change, if our chemistry is off, if our health is threatened, or if our self-image has been marred, the barometer can plunge—straight into despondency or depression.

If you asked the first five people you saw on the street, you would most likely get five different definitions of what it means to be happy.

"I'd be happy just to get rid of this horrible cold!"
"If I could land this new job, I know I'd be happy."
"If he would just ask me to marry him, I'd be the happiest woman in the world."
"I'd be happy if I could finally get around these rules and restrictions—if they would just let me do what I want to do!"
"I'd be totally happy if only I could have a new home."

Well...

The cold went away—but now you have a toothache!
You got that job—but you can't endure one more day of your new boss!
He asked you to marry him—but now you fervently wish you were single!
You got around those bothersome rules—but you've also suffered some hard consequences.
The new house got built—but it's nothing like you thought it would be.
It all seems like a terrible mistake.

Have any of those showers rained on your circumstances lately? Has happiness been a flighty, unstable companion to you, a fair-weather friend who bolts at the first sign of a storm cloud or a bumpy road?

I understand. But let me assure you of one thing, Beloved. That kind of happiness will never stay by your side. That kind of happiness isn't worth pursuing because frankly it isn't true happiness at all. That kind of happiness—the sort that depends on constantly fluctuating circumstances—is nothing more than the world's cheap imitation of the real thing.

The real happiness you desire is not an illusive dream because what you are craving is actually not happiness, which depends upon circumstances, but blessedness, which takes you through every circumstance.

In the weeks to come, as you give yourself wholeheartedly to this study and diligently apply what you learn, I can say with all confidence you will find what the world calls *happiness*. True happiness. Lasting happiness. The genuine article—a blessedness—that will sustain you and stand with you through the years of your life, *no matter what your circumstances are.*

How can I be so confident in what I am about to share with you? It's simply because I know the truth of God's Word. And I know the Sermon on the Mount has the shining key to unlock the gate to a wide, green estate of blessedness, which brings lasting happiness.

What we want when we say we want to be happy is disguised under the term *blessed* or *blessedness,* from the Greek word *makarios*. In this term the Greeks saw a moral element. Of course, it left God out, but they did understand that you had to behave or "fate" would punish you. In later years, the word *blessed* came to mean an inward correctness as an essence of happiness. Finally, in the Word of God *makarios* blossomed into beautiful truth. In the Scriptures *blessedness* means "a sense of God's approval." The term described "a happiness that came from pure character [which saw] sin as the fountainhead of all misery and holiness as the effectual cure for every woe."[1]

What you and I seek comes from being right with God.

The contentment we desire comes from doing what is right in His sight.

This, then, is "true" happiness. It is an enduring, flowering plant that draws its life and beauty and fragrance not from the shifting ground of circumstances but from being solidly, deeply rooted in a right relationship with God Himself. This explains why certain individuals can go through the most horrifying circumstances and heartbreaking experiences and yet maintain a peace, quietness, and confidence through it all. They seem happy in the midst of the storm.

Take time now to look at four scriptures that use the term *makarios* in one form or another. As you read them, keep in mind that the word *blessed* is God's word for true happiness. Be sure to write down the insights you glean from each verse:

 JOHN 13:17

"If you know these things, you are blessed if you do them."

 JOHN 20:29

Jesus said to him, "Because you have seen Me, have you believed? Blessed are they who did not see, and yet believed."

◗ ROMANS 14:22

(The word translated *happy* is the word *blessed.*)

The faith which you have, have as your own conviction before God. Happy is he who does not condemn himself in what he approves.

◗ 1 TIMOTHY 1:11

According to the glorious gospel of the blessed God, with which I have been entrusted.

Were you surprised by what you found in 1 Timothy 1:11? God is a blessed God. Doesn't it seem logical then, that the true happiness you crave would be found in drawing near to Him and actually becoming like Him?

Perhaps you say, "Oh, Kay, I don't see how I could ever be like God. If you only knew my past! If you only knew what I'm really like!"

Yes, Beloved, I do know what you are like because I know what I'm like apart from God and His lavish grace bestowed on me. (I'll tell you later in our study this week.) In tomorrow's study we'll look closely at the very first step in becoming like Him. It all begins with a heart attitude the Bible calls "poor in spirit."

– D A Y   T W O –

When you stop to think about it, aren't you thankful that true happiness comes from within—and not from without? As He begins the Sermon on the Mount, the Lord Jesus Christ tells us eight times in nine verses that blessedness is found in *who we are*. It is a blessedness that comes from being poor in spirit, mourning, being meek, hungering and thirsting after righteousness, being merciful, being pure in heart, being peacemakers, and even from being persecuted!

That last one seems especially strange, doesn't it? *We should be blessed—truly happy—because we're persecuted?* You couldn't get much further from the world's definition of happiness.

Is it any wonder that Jesus' teaching in the Sermon on the Mount so amazed His listeners? They were stunned. Their mouths dropped open. They couldn't believe their ears. Here was a man who spoke with ringing authority, a man who was God in the flesh. Here was the mighty Creator of all speaking to His created ones, telling them that the wellspring of what they craved was found in a sense of His approval.

Yes, friends and loved ones may belittle and ridicule our words and our choices, but what does it matter as long as God continually whispers, *"I know who you are, My child, and it brings Me pleasure."* Man, after all, was made for God's glory, God's pleasure. How then can man be complete or satisfied until he achieves that for which he was created?

Keeping all this in mind, let's look together at these amazing Beatitudes. As you read them, you will quickly become aware that they are not "natural" qualities. They couldn't be! How could a human heart— described in Jeremiah 17:9 as "deceitful and desperately wicked" (KJV)— attain these things unless God Himself opened the way?

Those who say that this Sermon is "not for today" have surely never understood what it means to be poor in spirit. This first beatitude is the foundation stone upon which all the others are built. It's the "alpha" of the Christian life and the "omega" to self-achievement. The sum of life is truly hidden in these opening words: "Blessed are the poor in spirit, for theirs is the kingdom of heaven."

What does it mean to be "poor in spirit"?

The word for *poor* means "one who crouches and cowers." It comes from a word which means "to cower down" or to "to hide one's self for fear." It means to be poverty-stricken, powerless, utterly destitute. Destitute of what? Destitute of the Spirit.

Humanity truly is poor in spirit—poor beyond our reckoning. Yet men and women outside of Christ neither acknowledge it nor even recognize it. What actually happened back in the Garden of Eden? Scripture says that in the moment Adam and Eve sinned, they *died*. But in what sense? Not physically—they didn't topple over on the spot. Nor did their souls die in that instant. They were still "living souls." Therefore, they must have died in another way, for God had clearly said that "in the day that you eat from it [that tree] you shall surely die" (Genesis 2:17).

In what sense, then, did the first man and woman die? We know that *something* happened immediately, because of the great changes that took place. Adam suddenly wanted to hide from the God he used to walk and talk with. He no longer wanted to be near his God. He suddenly had knowledge of good and evil. He realized he was naked and tried to clothe himself. He and his wife were forced to flee from the Garden in shame and fear.

Why? What happened?

I believe that man was created body, soul, and spirit. Although some people hold that man is a two-part being, to me Scripture shows us otherwise. In 1 Thessalonians 5:23 we read, "Now may the God of peace Himself sanctify you entirely; and may your *spirit* and *soul* and *body* be preserved complete, without blame at the coming of our Lord Jesus Christ" (italics added).

When man sinned, something did die immediately. There was a separation. Man was separated from God's Spirit. When man returns to God and receives Jesus as his Savior, he is spiritually reborn. The Holy Spirit comes to live within him, and he becomes a partaker of the "renewing by the Holy Spirit" (Titus 3:5).

What then is man apart from God? He is poor in spirit. He is utterly destitute. He lacks that connection with the Spirit who can commune with God and satisfy God, for who but God alone can satisfy God?

Who can begin to understand the things of God except the Spirit of God (1 Corinthians 2:11)?

To be poor in spirit, then, is to *realize* what state you are in before God. It is to be actively conscious of your total inability to walk with Him, please Him, or serve Him. To be poor in spirit is to abandon all pretense and to acknowledge your TOTAL dependence upon God for vindication from your sins. To be poor in spirit is to cry out with the apostle Paul, "I know that nothing good dwells in me, that is, in my flesh" (Romans 7:18).

Poverty of spirit is beautifully illustrated for us in Luke 18:9-14. Read this passage, printed out for you. Then, in your own words, explain how this parable illustrates what it means to be "poor in spirit." Note Jesus' *reasons* for telling this story, His reference to righteousness, and how He contrasts the two men. It might help you, after reading the passage, to make a list of what you observe about each of these men.

◗ LUKE 18:9-14

And He also told this parable to certain ones who trusted in themselves that they were righteous, and viewed others with contempt: "Two men went up into the temple to pray, one a Pharisee, and the other a tax-gatherer. The Pharisee stood and was praying thus to himself, 'God, I thank Thee that I am not like other people: swindlers, unjust, adulterers, or even like this tax-gatherer. I fast twice a week; I pay tithes of all that I get.' But the tax-gatherer, standing some distance away, was even unwilling to lift up his eyes to heaven, but was beating his breast, saying, 'God, be merciful to me, the sinner!' I tell you, this man went down to his house justified rather than the other; for everyone who exalts himself shall be humbled, but he who humbles himself shall be exalted."

FIRST MAN: THE _____   SECOND MAN: THE _____

Let me ask you a question, Beloved. Have you ever really seen your poverty of spirit? Have you ever seen yourself as a sinner? Have you realized your total inability to please God? Think on this and write your insights below.

— D A Y   T H R E E —

I was reared in a churchgoing family, and yet I wasn't truly saved until I was twenty-nine.

If you had asked me if I was a Christian during those earlier years, I would have told you yes, without hesitation. After all, I had been baptized and confirmed. I had taught Sunday school. I could even pray without a prayer book! My father became a minister, and my first husband, who is now deceased, studied for the ministry.

"Me? A Christian? Of course I am! After all, I live in the United States of America, and I attend church every Sunday. As a matter of fact, I think God is rather lucky to have me on His team! Here I am, this sweet young thing serving on the Ladies Auxiliary with all these old ladies!"

That's exactly the way I viewed myself. I actually credited God with good taste for choosing me. Poverty of spirit? I had no idea what it was. Until my late twenties, I really didn't have any great consciousness of sin. I had grown up in a religious environment yet had never heard the Word of God expounded in power, under the conviction of the Holy Spirit. I had a set of rules, obeyed them—and made sure people realized what a devout and obedient young lady I was!

Yet my heart was not right. No, far from it.

At the age of twenty-six I divorced my husband, took my two sons, and moved to the Washington, D.C., area. I stood in my living room, free of marital restraints, shook my fist at God, and said, "To hell with You, God. I'll see You around town. I'm going to go out and find someone who will love me."

I put on a low-cut dress, threw my mink stole over my shoulders, and went out to find someone to love me as my husband had not loved me—unconditionally. I wanted a man who would love me whether I was pretty or ugly, well or sick, happy or sad. In the process, I became what I had vowed I would never become—an immoral woman. I went from one man to another, looking for my "ideal." And my two little boys would ask over and over, "Mommy, is he going to be our daddy?"

The sweet, upright minister's daughter was wedged tight in a vise of sin.

Psalm 9:15 says that the heathen have sunk down into a pit that they have dug with their own hands. More and more I became aware of the pit into which I had sunk and the mud in which I was wallowing. Actually, I hated being so dirty. I wanted to be free. I wanted to climb out of that pit. After yet one more immoral encounter, I would say to myself, *That is so wrong. I am never, never going to do that again.*

But I would anyway. I would lose my grip, and there was that old mud waiting to welcome me back.

You could have seen my finger marks on the side of that muddy pit, where I had tried to claw my way out again and again. But try as I might, and in spite of all the resolve, will, and determination I could muster, I could not get out. I was trapped. How well I understand Paul's lament in Romans chapter 7: "For that which I am doing, I do not understand; for I am not practicing what I would like to do, but I am doing the very thing I hate." It was a horrible, horrible feeling. The good I wanted to do, I did not do—but instead I practiced the very evil I did not wish to do (see Romans 7:15,18-19).

Where once I thought God was lucky to have me on His team, now I wondered how He could even bear the sight of me. I knew that if I were to stand before Him, in justice He would have to say, "Depart from Me."

I wanted to be good, but for all my trying, I couldn't. I was utterly destitute. A beggar before God. I didn't know those words of Paul then, but someday later when I read them, I understood them fully. Paul's cry was my cry: "Wretched man that I am! Who will set me free from the body of this death?" (Romans 7:24).

On the morning of July 16, 1963, I ran to my room, flung myself at His feet, and cried out, "Oh God, I don't care what You do to me. I don't care if You paralyze me from the neck down…or if I never see another man for as long as I live…I don't care what You do to my two sons, if You'll just give me peace."

And in that moment I understood what it meant to be poor in spirit.

I had fallen to my knees an adulteress. I rose from my knees like a brand-new virgin—pure and clean. I received Jesus Christ, and I received His Holy Spirit, who took up residence within me. Life was going to be very different. I had taken the first step toward true happiness.

> The cords of death encompassed me,
> And the terrors of Sheol came upon me;
> I found distress and sorrow.
> Then I called upon the name of the LORD:
> "O LORD, I beseech Thee, save my life!"
>
> Gracious is the LORD, and righteous;
> Yes, our God is compassionate.
> The LORD preserves the simple;
> I was brought low, and He saved me.
> Return to your rest, O my soul,
> For the LORD has dealt bountifully with you.

For Thou hast rescued my soul from death,
My eyes from tears,
My feet from stumbling....

What shall I render to the LORD
For all His benefits toward me?
I shall lift up the cup of salvation,
And call upon the name of the LORD.
I shall pay my vows to the LORD,
Oh may it be in the presence of all His people....
Oh LORD, surely I am Thy servant,
I am Thy servant, the son [the daughter] of Thy handmaid,
Thou hast loosed my bonds.
(Psalm 116:3-8,12-14,16)

I had become poor in spirit! The kingdom of heaven was mine! God's Spirit had come within. Now my body was His temple. He had loosed my bonds that chained me to sin.

What is poverty of spirit? It is an absence of self-assurance, self-reliance, and pride. It is the deepest form of repentance. It is turning from your independence to total dependence upon God. It is brokenness.

Listen, my friend, as difficult as it might be to receive right now, you ought to open your arms and welcome *anything* that will break you, that will bend your knees, that will bring you to utter destitution before your God.

Blessed are the poor in spirit!

Let me give you two short assignments which will help affirm this.

1. Read Matthew 9:10-13, which follows, and then write out your answers below.

And it happened that as He was reclining at the table in the house, behold many tax-gatherers and sinners came and were dining with Jesus and His disciples. And when the Pharisees saw this, they said to His disciples, "Why is your Teacher eating with the tax-gatherers and sinners?" But when He heard this, He said, "It is not those who are healthy who need a physician, but those who are sick. But go and learn what this means, 'I DESIRE COMPASSION, AND NOT SACRIFICE,' for I did not come to call the righteous, but sinners."

a. Why was Jesus Christ criticized?

b. By whom was He criticized?

c. Whom did Jesus come to call?

2. Read Luke 4:16-21, which follows.

And He came to Nazareth, where He had been brought up; and as was His custom, He entered the synagogue on the Sabbath, and stood up to read. And the book of the prophet Isaiah was handed to Him. And He opened the book, and found the place where it was written, "THE SPIRIT OF THE LORD IS UPON ME, BECAUSE HE ANOINTED ME TO PREACH THE GOSPEL TO THE POOR. HE HAS SENT ME TO

PROCLAIM RELEASE TO THE CAPTIVES, AND RECOVERY OF SIGHT TO THE BLIND, TO SET FREE THOSE WHO ARE DOWNTRODDEN, TO PROCLAIM THE FAVORABLE YEAR OF THE LORD." And He closed the book, and gave it back to the attendant, and sat down; and the eyes of all in the synagogue were fixed upon Him. And He began to say to them, "Today this Scripture has been fulfilled in your hearing."

a. Do you see any possible parallel between this passage and what we've been studying about being poor in spirit?

b. Where and how?

— *D A Y   F O U R* —

In his excellent little book on the Sermon on the Mount, D. A. Carson writes:

> In much contemporary evangelism, there is little concern for whether or not God will accept us, and much concern for whether or not we will accept Him. Little attention is paid to whether or not we please Him, and much to whether or not He pleases us....
> I would argue that the reason we are currently seeing such an embar-

rassingly high percentage of spurious conversions to Christ is precisely because we have not first taught people their need of Christ.[2]

Until people come to see their utter poverty of spirit, they are not ready for the kingdom of heaven. This is what John the Baptist sought to accomplish when he cried out, "Repent, for the kingdom of heaven is at hand" and then told the scribes and Pharisees who came to Him to bring forth fruit worthy of repentance (Matthew 3:2,8). Surely he had seen their unwillingness to leave behind their pride, their self-reliance, and their self-assurance. In all probability they, too, thought God was lucky to have such men on His team. Their self-righteousness was like an unyielding stone wall which kept them from seeing the righteousness that comes by faith.

What kind of gospel are we preaching? A gospel that brings men and women under the conviction of sin? A gospel that causes men and women to drop to their knees and cry out, "God, be merciful to me a sinner!"?

In a letter to a young man who wanted to know how to preach the gospel, John Wesley shared a very biblical approach—one from which we can learn much.

He says that whenever he arrived at any new place to preach the gospel, he began with a general declaration of the love of God. Then he preached "the Law" (by which he meant all of God's righteous standards and the penalty of disobedience) as searchingly as he could. This he kept up until a large proportion of his hearers found themselves under deep conviction of sin, beginning even to despair of the possibility of forgiveness from his holy God. Then, and only then, did he introduce the good news of Jesus Christ. Wesley explained the saving significance of Christ's person, ministry, death, and resurrection, and the wonderful truth that salvation is solely by God's grace, through faith.

Unless his audiences sensed that they were guilty, and quite helpless to save themselves, the wonder and availability of God's grace would leave them unmoved. Wesley adds that after quite a number had been converted he would mix in more themes connected with law. He did this to underline the truth that genuine believers hunger for experiential righteousness, and continue to acknowledge poverty of spirit, recognizing constantly that their acceptance with God depends always and only on Christ's sacrifice.[3]

Poverty of spirit is not to be some passing emotional experience or a one-time event in the life of a child of God. Rather, it is a whole way of life, a life of total dependence upon God. It is continually realizing that in and of yourself you could *never* please God. You could *never* meet His standards of righteousness. Only by God's gift of His Spirit and by walking in the Spirit can you please Him.

Will you pause now, Beloved, and consider a few things that might keep you from recognizing your poverty of spirit? Tomorrow we examine the walk of the poor in spirit.

Read the passages printed out for you and answer the questions that follow.

◗ ROMANS 10:1-3
Brethren, my heart's desire and my prayer to God for them is for *their* salvation. For I bear them witness that they have a zeal for God, but not in accordance with knowledge. For not knowing about God's righteousness, and seeking to establish their own, they did not subject themselves to the righteousness of God.

1. What kept many in Israel from seeing their poverty of spirit?

2. Were they saved or not? Support your answer from these three verses.

3. Do you see this happening today? If so, where? Illustrate your answer.

▶ 1 CORINTHIANS 1:18-22

For the word of the cross is to those who are perishing foolishness, but to us who are being saved it is the power of God. For it is written, "I WILL DESTROY THE WISDOM OF THE WISE, AND THE CLEVERNESS OF THE CLEVER I WILL SET ASIDE." Where is the wise man? Where is the scribe? Where is the debater of this age? Has not God made foolish the wisdom of the world? For since in the wisdom of God the world through its wisdom did not come to know God, God was well-pleased through the foolishness of the message preached to save those who believe. For indeed Jews ask for signs, and Greeks search for wisdom.

1. In this passage what keeps people from seeing their poverty of spirit?

2. Do you see how this could happen today? If so, explain your answer.

Do you remember the story of the rich, young ruler? Read it again in Mark 10:17-25.

MARK 10:17-25

And as He was setting out on a journey, a man ran up to Him and knelt before Him, and began asking Him, "Good Teacher, what shall I do to inherit eternal life?" And Jesus said to him, "Why do you call Me good? No one is good except God alone. You know the commandments, 'DO NOT MURDER, DO NOT COMMIT ADULTERY, DO NOT STEAL, DO NOT BEAR FALSE WITNESS, Do not defraud, HONOR YOUR FATHER AND MOTHER.'" And he said to Him, "Teacher, I have kept all these things from my youth up." And looking at him, Jesus felt a love for him, and said to him, "One thing you lack: go and sell all you possess, and give to the poor, and you shall have treasure in heaven; and come, follow Me." But at these words his face fell, and he went away grieved, for he was one who owned much property.

And Jesus, looking around, said to His disciples, "How hard it will be for those who are wealthy to enter the kingdom of God!"

And the disciples were amazed at His words. But Jesus answered again and said to them, "Children, how hard it is to enter the kingdom of God! It is easier for a camel to go through the eye of a needle than for a rich man to enter the kingdom of God."

1. According to this passage, what could keep people from the kingdom of heaven, from seeing their poverty of spirit?

2. Can you see why this would happen then—and even today? If so, write out your insights.

⬤ 1 CORINTHIANS 1:26-31

For consider your calling, brethren, that there were not many wise according to the flesh, not many mighty, not many noble; but God has chosen the foolish things of the world to shame the wise, and God has chosen the weak things of the world to shame the things which are strong, and the base things of the world and the despised, God has chosen, the things that are not, that He might nullify the things that are, that no man should boast before God. But by His doing you are in Christ Jesus, who became to us wisdom from God, and righteousness and sanctification, and redemption, that, just as it is written, "LET HIM WHO BOASTS, BOAST IN THE LORD."

1. How does this passage relate to poverty of spirit?

2. What do you boast in before God?

Can you identify influences or attitudes in your life that might be keeping you from seeing your true poverty of spirit? What are they? Wealth? Worldly wisdom? Strong natural abilities? Your own righteousness? If so, Beloved, then you must also know that these are the very things which will keep you from the kingdom of heaven. Scripture says only the poor in spirit possess the kingdom of heaven. Think about these things, and make notes below. We'll talk more about them tomorrow.

– D A Y   F I V E –

The Sermon on the Mount describes the righteous lifestyle of those who belong to the kingdom of heaven. The question is, "How can one attain such righteousness?" The Beatitudes are certainly not qualities that come naturally to us.

The humanly impossible demands of Matthew 5:21–7:12 can only be fulfilled by Jesus Christ. That's the reason Jesus begins the Sermon on the Mount where He does! Before we can learn anything else about the kingdom of heaven, we must realize how spiritually poor we are.

How do you become poor in spirit?

I believe it all begins with catching a glimpse of God.

When I see Him—really see Him—in His holiness, in His power, in His blazing purity, I see myself for what I am. And what I see isn't lovely at all.

This is just what happened to the prophet Isaiah. Read Isaiah 6:1-8, then take time to think through and answer the questions that follow.

❿ ISAIAH 6:1-8

In the year of King Uzziah's death, I saw the Lord sitting on a throne, lofty and exalted, with the train of His robe filling the temple. Seraphim stood above Him, each having six wings; with two he covered his face, and with two he covered his feet, and with two he flew. And one called out to another and said,

"Holy, Holy, Holy, is the LORD of hosts,

the whole earth is full of His glory."

And the foundations of the thresholds trembled at the voice of him who called out, while the temple was filling with smoke. Then I said,

"Woe is me, for I am ruined!

Because I am a man of unclean lips,

and I live among a people of unclean lips;

for my eyes have seen the King, the LORD of hosts."

Then one of the seraphim flew to me, with a burning coal in his hand which he had taken from the altar with tongs. And he touched my mouth with it and said, "Behold, this has touched your lips; and your iniquity is taken away, and your sin is forgiven." Then I heard the voice of the Lord, saying, "Whom shall I send, and who will go for Us?" Then I said, "Here am I. Send me!"

1. When did Isaiah see himself as he really was?

2. At what point did Isaiah experience God's cleansing, His forgiveness?

3. When was Isaiah ready to do what God wanted him to do?

God shows us our poverty of spirit when we try, in our own strength, to walk in a way pleasing to God...and yet continually fail. This is the testimony the apostle Paul gives of his own experience in Romans 7. Humility came only when the once-proud Pharisee fell on his face and cried out, "Wretched man that I am! Who will set me free from the body of this death?" (Romans 7:24). Then God gave him the Spirit, and with the gift of the indwelling Spirit of God came the right to be called a son of God (Romans 8:1-17).

The Holy Spirit is the key to the Christian life. You attain salvation by realizing your utter spiritual poverty and turning to Jesus Christ. And you live the Christian life by remembering that apart from God's Spirit, you can do nothing!

In all of the Beatitudes you will find Jesus Christ as our glorious Example, the Author or Leader of our faith (Hebrews 12:2). Fix your eyes on Him, Beloved. See how He walked in total poverty of spirit. Remember, Jesus was God, the mighty Sovereign of the universe. And yet while He walked as a man on earth, He lived in total dependence upon God.

Read the following scriptures, and in the space provided note the ways Jesus depended upon the Father.

▶ JOHN 8:26,28-29

"I have many things to speak and to judge concerning you, but He who sent Me is true; and the things which I heard from Him, these I speak to the world.… When you lift up the Son of Man, then you will know that I am He, and I do nothing on My own initiative, but I speak these things as the Father taught Me. And He who sent Me is with Me; He has not left Me alone, for I always do the things that are pleasing to Him."

▶ LUKE 6:12-13

And it was at this time that He went off to the mountain to pray, and He spent the whole night in prayer to God. And when day came, He called His disciples to Him; and chose twelve of them, whom He also named as apostles.

▶ MATTHEW 3:13-17

Then Jesus arrived from Galilee at the Jordan coming to John, to be baptized by him. But John tried to prevent Him, saying, "I have need to be baptized by You, and do You come to me?" But Jesus answering said to him, "Permit it at this time; for in this way it is fitting for us to fulfill all righteousness." Then he permitted Him. And after being baptized, Jesus went up immediately from the water; and behold, the heavens were opened, and he saw the Spirit of God descending as a dove, and coming upon Him, and behold, a voice out of the heavens, saying, "This is My beloved Son, in whom I am well-pleased."

It's interesting to note in Matthew 3:13-17 that before Jesus Christ ever began His public ministry, He was baptized because He wanted to fulfill "all righteousness." It was at His baptism that the Spirit of God descended upon Him as a dove.

We are to walk as Jesus walked. As He was totally dependent upon the Spirit, so we must depend on Him as well. The words we speak are to be God's words. We are not to rely on our own wisdom. It's foolish even to *think* or speculate apart from considering God's truth. The works we do are to be His works. All of our activities are to be directed by the Spirit of God.

In Ephesians 5:15 and 18, Paul cautions us to be careful how we walk, reminding us that we are to be filled with the Holy Spirit and under His control. The Holy Spirit was not given to us merely as a guarantee of our salvation but also as our Comforter, Helper, Teacher, and Guide. Listen to the Word of the Lord:

In Him, you also, after listening to the message of truth, the gospel of your salvation—having also believed, you were sealed in Him with the

Holy Spirit of promise, who is given as a pledge of our inheritance, with a view to the redemption of God's own possession, to the praise of His glory. (Ephesians 1:13-14)

And I will ask the Father, and He will give you another Helper, that He may be with you forever;… But the Helper, the Holy Spirit, whom the Father will send in My name, He will teach you all things, and bring to your remembrance all that I said to you. (John 14:16,26)

But when He, the Spirit of truth, comes, He will guide you into all the truth; for He will not speak on His own initiative, but whatever He hears, He will speak; and He will disclose to you what is to come. (John 16:13)

To live in poverty of spirit is to let the Holy Spirit be to us all that He was to Jesus!

To walk in poverty of spirit means to abide in the Vine and to allow the life of the Vine, by God's Spirit, to flow through us so that we might bear fruit. For apart from Him we can do nothing (John 15:5).

To walk in poverty of spirit is to live out the truth of Philippians 2:12-13: "So then, my beloved, just as you have always obeyed, not as in my presence only, but now much more in my absence, work out your salvation with fear and trembling; for it is God who is at work in you, both to will and to work for His good pleasure."

To "work out your salvation" means to carry out to completion that which God desires to accomplish in you. And He will not only give you the ability to do it, He will give you the *will* to do it (Philippians 2:13). For this reason, walking in poverty of spirit means allowing God to have full rein within your life. To control you. It means going where He wants you to go. Saying all He wants you to say. Being all He wants you to be.

The bottom line? *Those who are poor in spirit walk in total dependence upon God.* Does that describe your life, as you read these words?

Years ago I had the privilege of teaching a short summer quarter at Columbia Bible College. During that time I became acquainted with Howard Ball, from Churches Alive. He was also teaching a course, and we enjoyed a sweet time of fellowship during those days. One afternoon as we were chatting, he told me how God had recently brought him up short with a simple question. And the question was this: "If God withdrew from you, from your church, from your ministry, what difference would it make?"

Howard looked at me and said softly, "Kay, I realized right then that I had lost my dependency upon God."

O Beloved, have you lost that which you once gained—that which laid the kingdom of heaven at your feet? Poverty of spirit is not to be a one-time affair. Rather, it is a way of life.

What is your prayer to God after considering these things? Write it out below. How blessed you are if you are poor in spirit!

MEMORY VERSE

"Blessed are the poor in spirit, for theirs is the kingdom of heaven."

MATTHEW 5:3

SMALL-GROUP DISCUSSION QUESTIONS

1. Define the word *blessed*. How does blessedness relate to happiness?
2. From where does the world think happiness comes? Why? From where does true happiness come?

3. What does it mean to be poor in spirit? What do the poor in spirit receive?

   a. Give an illustration from the Scriptures.

   b. How can a person come to see his poverty of spirit?

4. Why is it necessary to see and acknowledge your poverty of spirit? If you don't, what are you like? Can God bless that? Why?

5. Do you have attitudes or influences in your life that may keep you from recognizing your own poverty of spirit? How would your life be different if you made a decision to leave pride, self-assurance, and self-reliance behind?

6. In what ways can you relate to Paul's experience in Romans 7?

7. How do the poor in spirit live on a daily basis? How is Jesus our example?

DO YOU WEEP
OVER SIN?

— DAY ONE —

O nly a few of us had gathered for prayer meeting that Wednesday night.

But that didn't matter to me.

I was *so* hungry! As a brand-new child of God, I couldn't get enough of His Word. On Sunday mornings I sat in the sanctuary, elbows on the pew in front of me, eagerly drinking in the words of life. But I wanted more! That was why I found myself sitting among the "faithful few" in the dingy basement of a Reformed Presbyterian Church, with my Bible open in my lap.

The minister stood at a frail wooden podium and asked if someone might assist him by reading the scripture.

Nobody moved.

Nobody volunteered.

There wasn't a sound.

I felt embarrassed for this man of God. It must have been awful to stand up there and have no one respond. Finally I could stand it no longer. Although I was a new believer and a virtual stranger in the church, I volunteered.

"I'll read it," I said. I rose from my chair—feeling eyes staring into my back—went to the podium, opened my Bible, and began to read:

Now one of the Pharisees was requesting Him to dine with him. And He entered the Pharisee's house, and reclined at the table. And behold, there was a woman in the city who was a sinner; and when she learned that He was reclining at the table in the Pharisee's house, she brought an alabaster vial of perfume, and standing behind Him at His feet, weeping, she began to wet His feet with her tears, and kept wiping them with the hair of her head, and kissing His feet, and anointing them with the perfume. Now when the Pharisee who had invited Him saw this, he said to himself, "If this man were a prophet He would know who and what sort of person this woman is who is touching Him, that she is a sinner." And Jesus answered and said to him, "Simon, I have something to say to you." And he replied, "Say it, Teacher." "A certain moneylender had two debtors: one owed five hundred denarii, and the other fifty. When they were unable to repay, he graciously forgave them both. Which of them therefore will love him more?" Simon answered and said, "I suppose the one whom he forgave more." And He said to him, "You have judged correctly." And turning toward the woman, He said to Simon, "Do you see this woman? I entered your house; you gave Me no water for My feet, but she has wet My feet with her tears, and wiped them with her hair. You gave Me no kiss; but she, since the time I came in, has not ceased to kiss My feet. You did not anoint My head with oil, but she anointed My feet with perfume. For this reason I say to you, her sins, which are many, have been forgiven, for she loved much." (Luke 7:36-47)

Suddenly I was weeping.

Tears streamed down my face, and I could read no further. There, before this handful of strangers who had come to hear from God, I wept openly. I'd never read this passage before, but suddenly...*I was there*. I was in that Pharisee's house, washing the Teacher's feet with my tears, kissing them, and adoring the One who had radically transformed my life.

Empathy for this woman flooded my soul. The incident in Scripture may have been thousands of years old, but to me, it had just happened. How well I understood her love for the Lord. How I rejoiced with her in having her sins forgiven. Almost twenty centuries stood between us. We came from different cultures, different worlds, yet our sins were the same.

And so was our Lord.

There He stood. Jesus Christ…the same yesterday, today, and forever…granting both of us pardon. I was overwhelmed with love—and grief. How could I have sinned so grievously? How could I have wounded the One who loved me so much?

My tears kept falling and falling. The men and women in that dim little church basement sat in stunned silence, watching me, probably wondering what in the world could have triggered such an outburst. Little did they realize how fresh my forgiveness was.

Finally I regained control. Words came again. I had only three verses to go. Surely I could get through them.

"…but he who is forgiven little, loves little." And He said to her, "Your sins have been forgiven." And those who were reclining at the table with Him began to say to themselves, "Who is this man who even forgives sins?" And He said to the woman, "Your faith has saved you; go in peace." (Luke 7:47-50)

"Go in peace."

It was as though He was speaking directly to me. *"Go in peace, Daughter. Your faith has saved you."*

It was the very peace I had cried out for on July 16, 1963. "Oh, Lord, if You'll only give me peace!"

And He did. He not only gave me peace of heart, He gave me the Prince of Peace Himself, the God of all comfort. I had finally seen my sin as God saw it. I had abhorred it as God abhorred it. My heart was broken as His heart was broken, and in His great mercy He had heard my cry and forgiven my sin.

"Blessed are those who mourn," He said, "for they shall be comforted" (Matthew 5:4).

Do you understand, Beloved, what it means to mourn? Take a few minutes and read again Luke 7:36-50. Then write out below what you learn about Jesus, about the Pharisee, and about the woman. Note how each responds to the others.

JESUS   PHARISEE   WOMAN

In a sentence or two, explain which individual in this account you relate to most, and why.

— D A Y   T W O —

When was the last time you mourned—not because of what someone did to you or because of something that happened to you, but because what you did was wrong and it hurt God?

When was the last time you cried over the sins of others? When was the last time you hurt because God hurt? Is it hard for you to imagine a God who sits remotely in the heavens and yet truly hurts—in the depths of His great heart? When was the last time you wept in your prayers for others, lamenting over the awful degradation of humanity? Or the persecution of our brothers and sisters in Christ? Or that God's holy name had been mocked and blasphemed?

It's time for tears, Beloved. It's time to cry. It's time to pray, *"Oh God, break my heart with the things that break Your heart."*

Of all the "blesseds," "Blessed are those who mourn" may be the most difficult one for us to understand. What does mourning have to do with "blessedness"? What does grieving have to do with being spiritually prosperous or approved of God? How do tears and sorrow of heart link up with the true and lasting happiness you desire?

In God's economy, it all makes perfect sense.

For only those who mourn shall be comforted. The blessedness does not come in the mourning; it comes in the *results* of the mourning—knowing the comfort of His intimacy, the surety of His arms about you, hearing the beat of His heart as He draws you close to His all-sufficient breast.

The word for *mourn* in the second beatitude means "to mourn for or to lament as a way of life." The way the word is used here means that we are never to be hardened or inoculated to sin or sorrow. We are never to lose our ability to grieve, to weep, to mourn. We are never to become so calloused that we can look at sin or pain and remain unmoved—or even worse, laugh.

But *why* are we to mourn? Doesn't Scripture say the joy of the Lord is our strength? Yes, that is what Nehemiah 8:10 says, but we must never take that verse out of context.

The children of Israel had returned from captivity and rebuilt the temple and walls of Jerusalem. Now they were hearing the Word of God, the Word they had so neglected over the years as aliens in a strange land.

In their hearts they knew that very neglect had delivered them into captivity. But now the day of chastening was over. The seventy years of captivity had passed. It was no longer time to mourn or weep. It was time to receive the comfort of the Lord. Hence, the joy of the Lord could be their strength.

What do you see as you look around you today in our world? Is it a time for rejoicing in our nation? Is it a time for rejoicing across the world? Look at the condition of men's and women's hearts. Look at the complacency, the apathy within the church. Do you see men and women wholly consecrated to God? Do you see them hungering and thirsting after righteousness? Do you see them pursuing holiness? Do you see Peters and Pauls...or scribes and Pharisees?

If Jesus were here again in bodily form, if He were to walk through the inner city, down the avenues of entertainment, listen to the conversation in country clubs, peek behind the doors of hotel rooms, sit with us at our tables, listen to us in our bedrooms, do you think He would be mourning or rejoicing? If we are to be as He was in this world, we need to know the mind and the heart of God in regard to a society like ours.

Read the scriptures which follow.

As you read Isaiah 53:1-6, think about the second beatitude. Then write out how you think Jesus would respond to a society like ours, and why.

❯ ISAIAH 53:1-6

> Who has believed our message?
> And to whom has the arm of the LORD been revealed?
> For He grew up before Him like a tender shoot,
> And like a root out of parched ground;
> He has no stately form or majesty
> That we should look upon Him,
> Nor appearance that we should be attracted to Him.
> He was despised and forsaken of men,

A man of sorrows, and acquainted with grief;
And like one from whom men hide their face,
He was despised, and we did not esteem Him.

Surely our griefs He Himself bore,
And our sorrows He carried;
Yet we ourselves esteemed Him stricken,
Smitten of God, and afflicted.
But He was pierced through for our transgressions,
He was crushed for our iniquities;
The chastening for our well-being fell upon Him,
And by His scourging we are healed.
All of us like sheep have gone astray,
Each of us has turned to his own way;
But the LORD has caused the iniquity of us all
To fall on Him.

 GENESIS 6:1-12

Now it came about, when men began to multiply on the face of the land, and daughters were born to them, that the sons of God saw that the daughters of men were beautiful; and they took wives for themselves, whomever they chose. Then the LORD said, "My Spirit shall not strive with man forever, because he also is flesh; nevertheless his days shall be one hundred and twenty years." The Nephilim were on the earth in those days, and also afterward, when the sons of God came in to the daughters of men, and they bore children to them. Those were the mighty men who were of old, men of renown.

Then the LORD saw that the wickedness of man was great on the earth, and that every intent of the thoughts of his heart was only evil continually. And the LORD was sorry that He had made man on the earth, and He was grieved in His heart. And the LORD said, "I will blot out man whom I have created from the face of the land, from man to animals to creeping things and to birds of the sky; for I am sorry that I have made them." But Noah found favor in the eyes of the LORD.

These are the records of the generations of Noah. Noah was a righteous man, blameless in his time; Noah walked with God. And Noah became the father of three sons: Shem, Ham, and Japheth. Now the earth was corrupt in the sight of God, and the earth was filled with violence. And God looked on the earth, and behold, it was corrupt; for all flesh had corrupted their way upon the earth.

1. List what you learn about the state of humanity during this time.

2. How did the state of God's creation affect the heart of God? Record your answer.

● EZEKIEL 6:9

Then those of you who escape will remember Me among the nations to which they will be carried captive, how I have been hurt by their adulterous hearts which turned away from Me, and by their eyes, which played the harlot after their idols.

1. What is the condition of God's people as described in this verse?

2. How has it affected God?

Do you think it is a time to mourn in our nation? Why, or why not?

Would you be willing to pray, "God, break my heart with the things that break Your heart"? Why do you answer as you do?

— D A Y   T H R E E —

As we have seen from the second beatitude, mourning is not a one-time event. It is to be a habit of life while we are here upon the earth.

Does this seem strange to you? Let's think back to the life of the Lord Jesus and the times Scripture tells us that He wept.

He wept over Jerusalem, because they did not understand their day of opportunity…and terrible destruction awaited them.

And when He approached, He saw the city and wept over it, saying, "If you had known in this day, even you, the things which make for peace!

But now they have been hidden from your eyes. For the days shall come upon you when your enemies will throw up a bank before you, and surround you, and hem you in on every side, and will level you to the ground and your children within you, and they will not leave in you one stone upon another, because you did not recognize the time of your visitation." (Luke 19:41-44)

He wept at the tomb of Lazarus. There He stood—the Resurrection and the Life—in the shadow of death. Touched with the feeling of our infirmities, He wept freely, perhaps grieving over sin's deadly wages, paid again and again and again.

When Jesus therefore saw her weeping, and the Jews who came with her, also weeping, He was deeply moved in spirit, and was troubled, and said, "Where have you laid him?" They said to Him, "Lord, come and see." Jesus wept. And so the Jews were saying, "Behold how He loved him!" But some of them said, "Could not this man, who opened the eyes of him who was blind, have kept this man also from dying?" Jesus therefore again being deeply moved within, came to the tomb. Now it was a cave, and a stone was lying against it. (John 11:33-38)

For the wages of sin is death, but the free gift of God is eternal life in Christ Jesus our Lord. (Romans 6:23)

He wept and lamented over the blindness of Israel and the fate of Jerusalem. For there He stood with outstretched arms, and yet His own people would not come to Him that they might have life.

"O Jerusalem, Jerusalem, who kills the prophets and stones those who are sent to her! How often I wanted to gather your children together, the way a hen gathers her chicks under her wings, and you were unwilling. Behold, your house is being left to you desolate! For I say to you, from now on you shall not see Me until you say, 'BLESSED IS HE WHO COMES IN THE NAME OF THE LORD!'" (Matthew 23:37-39)

Surely it was grief that drove Him to a lonely place by Himself when He heard how John the Baptist's head was delivered on a platter to Herod and Herodias. Sin had seemingly silenced righteousness by cutting off the head of the one who had said, "It is not lawful for you to have her" (Matthew 14:4). If only they had listened to John, they might have found forgiveness. And had he lived, John might have pointed many more to the Way, the Truth, and Life. But John's courageous voice had been silenced, and Jesus wanted some time and space to be alone with His Father (Matthew 14:13).

Yes, Jesus was a Man of Sorrows. Righteousness could not laugh in the presence of sin. He mourned. And if He mourned, then my heart must also break with the things that break God's heart. I, too, must mourn.

But over what are we to mourn? I would like us to consider three things in these next three days on this beatitude.

• First, we are to mourn over sin in our own lives.
• Second, we are to mourn over sin in the church.
• And third, we are to mourn over sin in the world.

There is a specific progression to the Beatitudes. As I have mentioned, the foundation is poverty of spirit. All else finds its footing there. Sin is independence from God; it is the opposite of being poor in spirit. But when that true poverty of spirit comes, then righteous mourning will rise up like walls on its foundation. Mourning and repentance go together. Remember, repentance is the deepest form of poverty of spirit.

We will be looking together at a passage from the book of 2 Corinthians. Before we read these verses, however, let's consider the setting of this book. The church at Corinth had sinned grievously. Because of that sin, Paul had sternly reprimanded them by means of a letter—1 Corinthians. Now, in 2 Corinthians, he expresses the sorrow he felt in having to write that first letter. This sorrow, however, has turned to rejoicing because of their repentant response. In the midst of all this, God gives us an insight into two kinds of sorrow and the fruit of each.

Read 2 Corinthians 7:6-13, marking in two distinctive ways the two kinds of sorrow mentioned in the passage. In the right-hand margin beside the passage, note where each kind of sorrow leads.

▶ 2 CORINTHIANS 7:6-13

6 But God, who comforts the depressed, comforted us by the coming of Titus;

7 and not only by his coming, but also by the comfort with which he was comforted in you, as he reported to us your longing, your mourning, your zeal for me; so that I rejoiced even more.

8 For though I caused you sorrow by my letter, I do not regret it; though I did regret it—for I see that that letter caused you sorrow, though only for a while—

9 I now rejoice, not that you were made sorrowful, but that you were made sorrowful to the point of repentance; for you were made sorrowful according to the will of God, in order that you might not suffer loss in anything through us.

10 For the sorrow that is according to the will

of God produces a repentance without regret, leading to salvation; but the sorrow of the world produces death.

11 For behold what earnestness this very thing, this godly sorrow, has produced in you: what vindication of yourselves, what indignation, what fear, what longing, what zeal, what avenging of wrong! In everything you demonstrated yourselves to be innocent in the matter.

12 So although I wrote to you it was not for the sake of the offender, nor for the sake of the one offended, but that your earnestness on our behalf might be made known to you in the sight of God.

13 For this reason we have been comforted.

Now go back and mark in a third way each occurrence of the word *comfort*. Note in the margin when the comfort came.

Now, Beloved, what kind of sorrow do you experience when you sin? There is a worldly sorrow, a sorrow that says, "I'm sorry I got caught! I'm sorry I have to pay the price for my sin." This sorrow focuses on self and simply moans over the personal consequences of its own sin. It is so totally self-centered that it never thinks about how sin affects the heart of God. And where does this sorrow lead? It leads to death because it does not lead to repentance.

The other sorrow mentioned is godly sorrow, which leads to repentance. Remember, repentance is a change of mind that results in regret and thus produces a change in direction. This kind of sorrow brings salvation. The salvation Paul is talking about in this passage is not a salvation that saves us from hell and takes us to heaven. Rather, it is salvation from the snares of sin. Godly sorrow causes us to run to the arms of God, weeping, confessing our sin. And He meets us in that moment, just as He has promised.

> If we confess our sins, He is faithful and righteous to forgive us our sins and to cleanse us from all unrighteousness. (1 John 1:9)

The comfort of God awaits us because we have mourned as God would have us mourn. The cleansing from *all* unrighteousness comes, covering even what we did not remember or know to confess. Why? Because God sees our heart, and our heart is to be right with our Holy Father.

In 2 Samuel 11, God gives us a vivid illustration of sin's consuming passion. David, God's chosen king, had apparently slipped into a period of midlife apathy. Scripture tells us that David had not gone to war at a time when other kings were marching off to battle. Idle and restless, David allowed himself to fall into a vicious whirlpool of sin that spun him round and round, taking him deeper and deeper into the waters of iniquity. He might have drowned then and there, had it not been for the courageous obedience of Nathan, the prophet—a man of God who stood between the king and an abyss.

From his rooftop one balmy evening David saw a beautiful woman bathing—and did not turn away! He knew this was the wife of one of his faithful soldiers, a soldier serving his king who was absent from the field of battle, but he took her anyway. Although he had wives and concubines of his own, his lust was fully engaged. He had to possess Bathsheba.

When the news came that Bathsheba was pregnant, David missed a huge opportunity to repent. Instead of running to the throne of mercy with his sin, he allowed himself to be drawn even deeper into deceit. He plotted how to bring her husband, Uriah, home from battle so that Uriah would sleep with Bathsheba and thus suppose the child was his. David didn't know what nobility he was dealing with, for Uriah wouldn't consider sleeping with his wife while his fellow soldiers were still on the field of battle! Even though David made Uriah drunk, still Uriah stood—a man of principle. Surely David winced in the presence of such righteousness.

Once again David failed to admit and mourn for his sin. As a result he fell even further. His intention for Uriah was obvious when he wrote a letter to his commander, Joab: "Place Uriah in the front line of the fiercest battle and withdraw from him, so that he may be struck down and die" (2 Samuel 11:15). The whirlpool was getting smaller, tighter, stronger. When Joab sent the news of the lives lost—including that of loyal Uriah—David merely clucked his tongue.

> Then David said to the messenger, "Thus you shall say to Joab, 'Do not let this thing displease you, for the sword devours one as well as another; make your battle against the city stronger and overthrow it.'" (2 Samuel 11:25)

Bathsheba mourned for her husband, but David had a new wife. He didn't mourn. He didn't weep. In his sin-darkened thoughts, he imagined that he had neatly resolved his own sin. He believed he had tied off all those messy loose ends. Little did he realize that his very life would soon begin to unravel.

Apparently David had forgotten that a holy God cannot overlook sin, even the sin of God's anointed king.

Years ago I heard my pastor, Wayne Barber, make these three statements, and I wrote them in my Bible:

- Sin will take you farther than you ever thought you would stray.
- Sin will keep you longer than you ever thought you would stay.
- Sin will cost you more than you ever thought you would pay.

If you have ever been drawn into the whirlpool of sin, you know how true these statements are.

It wasn't until David was confronted by God's prophet that he began to mourn with a godly sorrow. How thankful I am that God not only shares with us the victories of His saints but also their shameful defeats. "For whatever was written in earlier times was written for our instruction, that through perseverance and the encouragement of the Scriptures we might have hope" (Romans 15:4).

Read through Psalm 51:1-17 and mark every reference to sin and its synonyms—evil, iniquity, transgressions.

◗ PSALM 51:1-17

1 Be gracious to me, O God, according to Thy lovingkindness;

According to the greatness of Thy compassion blot out my transgressions.

2 Wash me thoroughly from my iniquity,

And cleanse me from my sin.

3 For I know my transgressions,

And my sin is ever before me.

4 Against Thee, Thee only, I have sinned,

And done what is evil in Thy sight,

So that Thou art justified when Thou dost speak,

And blameless when Thou dost judge.

5 Behold, I was brought forth in iniquity,

And in sin my mother conceived me.

6 Behold, Thou dost desire truth in the innermost being,

And in the hidden part Thou wilt make me know wisdom.

7 Purify me with hyssop, and I shall be clean;

Wash me, and I shall be whiter than snow.

8 Make me to hear joy and gladness,

Let the bones which Thou hast broken rejoice.

9 Hide Thy face from my sins,

And blot out all my iniquities.

10 Create in me a clean heart, O God,

And renew a steadfast spirit within me.

11 Do not cast me away from Thy presence,

And do not take Thy Holy Spirit from me.

12 Restore to me the joy of Thy salvation,

And sustain me with a willing spirit.

13 Then I will teach transgressors Thy ways,

And sinners will be converted to Thee.

14 Deliver me from bloodguiltiness, O God, Thou God of my salvation;

Then my tongue will joyfully sing of Thy righteousness.

15 O Lord, open my lips,

That my mouth may declare Thy praise.

16 For Thou dost not delight in sacrifice, otherwise I would give it;

Thou art not pleased with burnt offering.

17 The sacrifices of God are a broken spirit;

A broken and a contrite heart, O God, Thou wilt not despise.

What do you learn from this psalm about David's repentance?

David had at last faced and admitted the ghastly depths of his own sin. Broken and crushed by grief, he fell on his face before heaven.

He was finally a candidate for the comfort of the Lord.

Centuries later, James would describe the very process David must have gone through in his repentance and restoration.

Submit therefore to God. Resist the devil and he will flee from you. Draw near to God and He will draw near to you. Cleanse your hands, you sinners; and purify your hearts, you double-minded. Be miserable and mourn and weep; let your laughter be turned into mourning, and your joy to gloom. Humble yourselves in the presence of the Lord, and He will exalt you. (James 4:7-10)

As we consider this portion of Scripture, let's remember James's stated purpose for writing this letter:

My brethren, if any among you strays from the truth, and one turns him back, let him know that he who turns a sinner from the error of his way will save his soul from death, and will cover a multitude of sins. (James 5:19-20)

In his epistle James shows us what the truth is—and then what it means to stray from that truth. Those of you who have worked through our Precept course on the book of James know the deep conviction that a study like this brings. Yet that conviction also brings great liberation. In James 4:7-10, James is calling people to repentance. They were caught up in a friendship with the world—a friendship that had made them proud, had led them into spiritual harlotry, and had broken the heart of God.

What is the solution?

It is to stop laughing at sin.

"Be miserable and mourn and weep," James writes in verse 9. "Let your laughter be turned into mourning, and your joy to gloom."

Is that the sort of attitude toward sin you see as you look around you today? Hardly!

You see people who chuckle, snicker, and laugh out loud over sin. The "humor" of sin is standard fare for almost every comedian, television series, and play on Broadway.

Recently, I was skimming an old *Reader's Digest* article on "how to stay young," by elderly comedian George Burns. (At age sixty-two, I notice articles like this!) If you ever heard the old George Burns and Gracie Allen programs on the radio, you will remember how funny this man can be. But those were different days, weren't they? The jokes were clean. Comedians didn't have to rely on constant sexual references or bathroom humor. You could listen with your whole family and feel good about it. In this article, however, Burns tainted his comments with frequent sexual innuendoes. I felt like washing my hands after replacing the magazine.

What is God's word to us? "Cleanse your hands, you sinners; and purify your hearts, you double-minded. Be miserable and mourn and weep" (James 4:8-9). How can we laugh over sin when sin nailed Jesus to the cross?

Have you sinned, Beloved? Can you be comforted? Note I said "can." To put it another way, have you placed yourself in a position where you can receive God's wonderful comfort? It all depends on whether or not you have His heart on the matter. It all depends on whether or not you have mourned!

Honestly before God determine what your attitude toward sin is. Are you willing to be changed? Write your thoughts out, and we will continue to consider sin's ways tomorrow.

– D A Y   F O U R –

The second object or cause for our mourning is sin in the church.

I'm going to ask you to pause and think something through for a minute or two. How does your church deal with sin? When sin is discovered within your congregation—adultery, verbal abuse, drunkenness, financial misdealings—does your church take action?

Do you feel it would be "judgmental" for a church to speak out on these matters, knowing that Jesus tells us in Matthew 7:1 that we are not to judge? (We're going to study this oft misquoted verse in *Lord, I'm Torn Between Two Masters*. You won't want to miss it.) Perhaps you find yourself reasoning, "Well, after all, we're all sinners! Besides, what would we *do* with someone who was openly sinning? Is it worth risking a lawsuit?"

These are logical, legitimate questions. It's certainly all right to ask such questions—as long as we honestly seek *biblical* solutions.

Read 1 Corinthians 5 and then write out your answers to the questions that follow. Mark each of the following words and their synonyms in a distinctive way or color: *mourned, immoral, so-called brother, judge.*

● 1 CORINTHIANS 5

¹ It is actually reported that there is immorality among you, and immorality of such a kind as does not exist even among the Gentiles, that someone has his father's wife.

² And you have become arrogant, and have not mourned instead, in order that the one who had done this deed might be removed from your midst.

³ For I, on my part, though absent in body but present in spirit, have already judged him who has so committed this, as though I were present.

⁴ In the name of our Lord Jesus, when you are assembled, and I with you in spirit, with the power of our Lord Jesus,

⁵ I have decided to deliver such a one to Satan for the destruction of his flesh, that his spirit may be saved in the day of the Lord Jesus.

⁶ Your boasting is not good. Do you not know that a little leaven leavens the whole lump of dough?

⁷ Clean out the old leaven, that you may be a new lump, just as you are in fact unleavened. For Christ our Passover also has been sacrificed.

⁸ Let us therefore celebrate the feast, not with old leaven, nor with the leaven of malice and wickedness, but with the unleavened bread of sincerity and truth.

⁹ I wrote you in my letter not to associate with immoral people;

¹⁰ I did not at all mean with the immoral people of this world, or with the

covetous and swindlers, or with idolaters; for then you would have to go out of the world.

11 But actually, I wrote to you not to associate with any so-called brother if he should be an immoral person, or covetous, or an idolater, or a reviler, or a drunkard, or a swindler—not even to eat with such a one.

12 For what have I to do with judging outsiders? Do you not judge those who are within the church?

13 But those who are outside, God judges. REMOVE THE WICKED MAN FROM AMONG YOURSELVES.

1. What was the problem in the church at Corinth? Why was Paul upset with them?

2. What were his instructions to them? List them one by one after reading the whole chapter.

3. Whom were they to judge?

4. Whom would God judge?

As you saw in 1 Corinthians 5, the thing which upset Paul most was not the son's incest but the church's arrogance about it! The church had not mourned over the sin. They had not shown a godly sorrow that led to repentance. (Remember 2 Corinthians 7 and your study on worldly sorrow versus godly sorrow? Sin had been tolerated instead of judged—until Paul wrote 1 Corinthians!)

"But," people have said to me, "if we put people out of our fellowship, they will just go deeper into sin! We have to show them the love of God! The forgiveness of God!"

Are we wiser, then, than God Himself? Do we know the ways of man better than the One who created man? Our responsibility, Beloved, is not to turn to human reasoning. Rather, our responsibility is to be obedient to God. And what does God's Word say? "Remove the wicked man from among yourselves" (1 Corinthians 5:13). Give him up to Satan for the destruction of his flesh. Don't have anything to do with him. Don't even eat with him. Yes, the guilty party may go deeper into sin. That's just what God meant when He directed Paul to write: "Deliver such a one to Satan for the destruction of his flesh" (1 Corinthians 5:5).

Why does God tell us to do this? So that man might come to an experiential knowledge of the awful wages of his sin and, feeling the just judgment of God, be brought to a godly sorrow and to repentance.

Did it work? Yes, it did if 2 Corinthians 2:5-11 refers to him. (Some believe it does; others believe it refers to another problem.) The church repented, the man repented, and Paul urged the congregation to forgive the man, comfort him, and reaffirm their love for him. We must never forget, Beloved, that God cannot forgive what we will not confess. And we cannot experience His comfort as long as we walk in rebellion.

Your next question may be, "But how do you approach a person?

How do you deal with a person who is living in sin?" The answer is spelled out clearly in Matthew 18:15-20. There you will find the steps you are to take when your brother or sister sins against you.

◗ MATTHEW 18:15-20

15 "And if your brother sins, go and reprove him in private; if he listens to you, you have won your brother.

16 "But if he does not listen *to you,* take one or two more with you, so that BY THE MOUTH OF TWO OR THREE WITNESSES EVERY FACT MAY BE CONFIRMED.

17 "And if he refuses to listen to them, tell it to the church; and if he refuses to listen even to the church, let him be to you as a Gentile and a tax-gatherer.

18 "Truly I say to you, whatever you shall bind on earth shall be bound in heaven; and whatever you loose on earth shall be loosed in heaven.

19 "Again I say to you, that if two of you agree on earth about anything that they may ask, it shall be done for them by My Father who is in heaven.

20 "For where two or three have gathered together in My name, there I am in their midst."

What does Jesus say?
- Go to him and reprove him in private.
- If he does not listen to you, then take one or two more with you, and bring it before the church.
- If he refuses to listen to the church, then you are to treat him as a Gentile and a tax-gatherer. In other words, have nothing to do with him.
- You have God's backing on such action. He is there among the two or three gathered in His name.

When you do this as a church body, you are binding on earth what has already been bound in heaven. You are carrying out the will of God on earth.

Isn't it interesting to see Matthew 18:18-19 in the light of its context? So often these verses are misquoted and wrenched out of context because people simply quote what they hear others say, or they do not carefully study the Word so as to handle it accurately. Therefore I commend you, my friend, for devoting the time and energy to study and grow. In so doing, you are fulfilling God's clear command: "Be diligent to present yourself approved to God as a workman who does not need to be ashamed, handling accurately the word of truth" (2 Timothy 2:15).

I want to show you one last passage today, and acquaint you with the heart of a man who knew how to mourn! Jeremiah deeply mourned over the sin of God's people. He has become known to generations of God's people as "the weeping prophet."

"Harvest is past, summer is ended,
And we are not saved."
For the brokenness of the daughter of my people I am broken;
I mourn, dismay has taken hold of me.
Is there no balm in Gilead?
Is there no physician there?
Why then has not the health of the daughter of my people been
    restored?

"O that my head were waters,
And my eyes a fountain of tears,
That I might weep day and night
For the slain of the daughter of my people!

"…For the mountains I will take up a weeping and wailing,
And for the pastures of the wilderness a dirge,
Because they are laid waste, so that no one passes through,
And the lowing of the cattle is not heard;
Both the birds of the sky and the beasts have fled; they are gone."

…Thus says the LORD of hosts,
"Consider and call for the mourning women, that they may come;
And send for the wailing women, that they may come!
"And let them make haste, and take up a wailing for us,
That our eyes may shed tears,
And our eyelids flow with water.
"For a voice of wailing is heard from Zion,
'How are we ruined!
We are put to great shame,
For we have left the land,
Because they have cast down our dwellings.'"
(Jeremiah 8:20-22; 9:1,10,17-19)

Should we not join Jeremiah in weeping over the sins of those who call themselves children of God? Let's call for mourners. Let's weep together and cry out to God. The Lord may hear us and attend to the words of our cry.

God's desires a chaste virgin as a bride for His Son (2 Corinthians 11:2). Not a harlot.

— D A Y   F I V E —

We are to mourn over our own sin and over sin in the church. But Scripture also tells us that we are to mourn over sin in our world.

Years ago Jack and I were enjoying our annual August days of rest and relaxation in the home of our dear friends Chuck and Barb Snyder in the Pacific Northwest. Taking care of the Arthurs has become a ministry with them! In the evenings we lingered over delicious meals and hours of even more delightful conversation. They are the kind of people you can really open up with, and their insights and perspectives through the years have been a treasure to Jack and me.

Jack usually takes the opportunity to go deep-sea fishing during our time together, and Chuck meets with those he's ministering to and takes care of his advertising business—which leaves Barb and me free to do all the fun "girl things" we like to do.

One afternoon as Barb and I came out of one of Nordstrom's unbelievable shoe sales, we noticed that the musical *Chorus Line* was playing. Seeing the show seemed like a fun prospect, so we bought tickets for the afternoon performance, never seriously considering whether or not the content might be offensive.

The musical opened with some great choreography that reminded me of how out of shape I was. Talk about stamina—they had it! All went well until the singing and dancing stopped and the dialogue began. One by one, each performer in the chorus line stepped forward to tell something about herself.

I couldn't believe what I was hearing! The words weren't just crude, they were utterly perverted, rash, and blatant. Truthfully, they mocked everything that was holy and righteous and pure. They reeked with filth. Their blatant sex-talk set off ripples of uncomfortable snickers across the audience. It wasn't that enjoyable, wholesome, belly-shaking laughter we all need to experience now and then, but insidious, sick, I-can't-believe-I'm-hearing-what-I'm-hearing sort of laughter. To my ears, it was filled with guilt.

I jammed my fingers into my ears and said right out loud, "Oh, Father, I am so sorry, so sorry." Barb and I turned to one another and agreed to get out of there immediately. We'd heard enough—and a great deal more than enough.

As we stood up to leave, I wanted to shout to everyone in the theater, "Why are you laughing? You know it's wrong! Why do you listen to such filth? This is what's destroying America." I wanted to tell them about a holy God who sees and knows all that we do and all that we think.

I wanted to, but I didn't.

Oh, Jeremiah, I know why you wept. Did I leave you standing alone? I honestly don't know what I should have done. All I know is that I didn't do what I wanted to do. A verse from Scripture sometimes restrains me in situations like that. I thought of Matthew 12:19, which tells us that Jesus did not cry out or raise His voice in the streets. I may have found myself casting my pearls before swine, giving what is holy to dogs. Or maybe, in my flesh, I was simply too weak to be a watchman on the walls warning the people to flee their sin (Ezekiel 33).

One thing I do know: My heart broke with the things that broke God's heart. And more and more as my heart draws closer to His, I feel, I weep, and I mourn over sin in the world.

Your last assignment for Day Five is to read Ezekiel 9, a short chapter containing only eleven verses.

The book of Ezekiel was written during the time of the Babylonian captivity of Judah. (Ezekiel was taken captive in 597 B.C. on the second siege.) God was sending the southern kingdom of Judah into captivity because the people had plunged headlong into idolatry, perversion, and total rebellion against His holy commandments. Through His prophets, God had constantly tried to call the people to repentance, but they had hardened their hearts and stopped their ears. They would not listen. At the time of Ezekiel 9, Jerusalem had not yet been totally destroyed. Some of the Jewish people were still living in the land, and God had yet to bring about a full execution of judgment upon the sacred city.

Now carefully read the chapter that follows, and in a distinctive way mark every occurrence of the word *mark*. Also mark the phrase "sigh and groan." Then answer the questions which follow the text.

▶ EZEKIEL 9

¹ Then He cried out in my hearing with a loud voice saying, "Draw near, O executioners of the city, each with his destroying weapon in his hand."

² And behold, six men came from the direction of the upper gate which faces north, each with his shattering weapon in his hand; and among them

was a certain man clothed in linen with a writing case at his loins. And they went in and stood beside the bronze altar.

3 Then the glory of the God of Israel went up from the cherub on which it had been, to the threshold of the temple. And He called to the man clothed in linen at whose loins was the writing case.

4 And the LORD said to him, "Go through the midst of the city, even through the midst of Jerusalem, and put a mark on the foreheads of the men who sigh and groan over all the abominations which are being committed in its midst."

5 But to the others He said in my hearing, "Go through the city after him and strike; do not let your eye have pity, and do not spare.

6 "Utterly slay old men, young men, maidens, little children, and women, but do not touch any man on whom is the mark; and you shall start from My sanctuary." So they started with the elders who were before the temple.

7 And He said to them, "Defile the temple and fill the courts with the slain. Go out!" Thus they went out and struck down the people in the city.

8 Then it came about as they were striking and I alone was left, that I fell on my face and cried out saying, "Alas, Lord GOD! Art Thou destroying the whole remnant of Israel by pouring out Thy wrath on Jerusalem?"

9 Then He said to me, "The iniquity of the house of Israel and Judah is very, very great, and the land is filled with blood, and the city is full of

perversion; for they say, 'The LORD has forsaken the land, and the LORD does not see!'

10 "But as for Me, My eye will have no pity nor shall I spare, but I shall bring their conduct upon their heads."

11 Then behold, the man clothed in linen at whose loins was the writing case reported, saying, "I have done just as Thou hast commanded me."

1. Why did the Lord summon the executioners? What was His purpose?

2. What were the executioners to do? (Note where they were to begin.)

3. What was the man clothed in linen with the writing case to do?

4. Why was he to do this?

5. Who was exempt from the judgment of the executioners? Why?

Hear me, Beloved. Unless America repents, God is going to have to judge us, and His means of judgment may be the same with us as with Jerusalem. He may bring another country to take us captive. If He were to do this, and if He were to send a man with a writing case to put a mark (a *tau*, which was the form of a cross) on the foreheads of those who sigh and groan over all the abominations committed in the United States of America, would He put a *tau* on your forehead? In that day God will be no respecter of persons. As in Israel He started from the temple and moved out to the people, so in America He will start in the churches and move from the leaders to the people. Judgment begins with the house of God.

None will be exempt. It will be a *tau* or a sword. Only the mourners will be spared.

Yes, Beloved, it's a time for tears. It's a time to cry, "Oh, God, break my heart with the things that break Your heart."

Together then, we may enjoy the comfort of God—so deep, so wide, so long, and so high that we could never put it into words.

MEMORY VERSE

Blessed are those who mourn, for they shall be comforted.

MATTHEW 5:4

SMALL-GROUP DISCUSSION QUESTIONS

1. Have the class quote Matthew 5:4. How would you explain this second beatitude to someone?
2. Why are those who mourn blessed?
3. Over what things are we to mourn?
4. How are you personally affected by your own sins? Discuss the two kinds of sorrow mentioned in 2 Corinthians 7. Have you experienced these two kinds of sorrow? What was the effect of each one?
5. How does sin in the church impact members of the body? What insights have you gained from 1 Corinthians 5 and Matthew 18:15-20?
6. How are you to respond to sin in the lives of others? What is the benefit of following the directive of Matthew 18:15-20?
7. What are your thoughts as you consider what is happening in our society and in our world? How does Ezekiel 9 relate to today's world?
8. What happens to discernment when God's people do not confront sin?
9. What place did mourning have in the life of Jesus?
10. What impressed you the most about this week's study?
11. Have the class share anything God is doing in their lives as a result of this study.

MEEKNESS IN THE PRESENCE OF SOVEREIGNTY

— D A Y   O N E —

A s you study the character traits described in the Beatitudes, you can't help but realize one thing: These are by no means "natural" qualities.

Poverty of spirit doesn't come naturally to you and me.

Mourning over sin doesn't come naturally.

Meekness doesn't come naturally.

Where, then, do these supernatural traits come from? They are woven in and through the fabric of our character on the loom of God's indwelling Holy Spirit. He is making our lives a tapestry that portrays the image of the living God.

We come to the third beatitude today. Having seen our total poverty of spirit, and having mourned over our independent lifestyle which brought such grief to the heart of God, in meekness we must kneel in total submission to Him. We must bow before the sovereign God and in purity of trust say, "What pleases You, my Father, pleases me."

It is the meek who will inherit the earth.

Tell this to the Alexanders, Napoleons, Hitlers, and Stalins of this world! They will laugh at you, call you insane, and "take counsel together against the LORD and against His Anointed" (Psalm 2:2). They march on, seeking to conquer the earth through cruelty and force of arms, for-getting that they are men and that their "days are determined, the number of [their] months is with [God], and [their] limits [God] hast set so that [they] cannot pass" (Job 14:5). They deliberately forget that the Lord Almighty rules, "In whose hand is the life of every living thing, and the breath of all mankind" (Job 12:10).

Meekness. What is it? How does it fit with the sovereignty and char-acter of God? These are the questions we want to answer this week as we continue to feast on the Sermon on the Mount.

Oftentimes *meek* or *meekness* is translated *gentle* or *gentleness* in the New American Standard Bible. W. E. Vine writes: "Meekness is an in-wrought grace of the soul; and the exercises of it are first and chiefly towards God. It is that temper of spirit in which we accept His dealings with us as good, and therefore without disputing and resisting."[1]

Meekness speaks of a submissive and trusting attitude toward God. It is an attitude which accepts all of God's ways with us as good. It does not murmur or dispute. It neither rebels nor retaliates. It realizes that what comes to us from the hand of man has been permitted by God's sover-eignty, has been filtered by His fingers of love, and will be used by God for His glory and our ultimate good.

Meekness looks beyond circumstances—no matter how upsetting and hurtful—and bows the knee to the sovereign God.

I am convinced, Beloved, that if we are to walk in meekness we must know our God. We must accept His sovereign rule. We must grapple with the character of this One who rules over the affairs of men and the hosts of heaven. Of all the truths I have ever learned, none has brought me more assurance, boldness, calmness, devotion, equilibrium, gratitude, and humility than this study of the sovereignty of God. I pray it will do the same for you.

To begin our study, let's turn once again to what I believe is the key-stone of all scriptures on God's sovereignty. As you read this passage, mark every reference to God, including the pronouns, with a △ .

● DANIEL 4:34-35

34 "But at the end of that period I, Nebuchadnezzar, raised my eyes toward heaven, and my reason returned to me, and I blessed the Most High and praised and honored Him who lives forever;

For His dominion is an everlasting dominion,

And His kingdom endures from generation to generation.

35 And all the inhabitants of the earth are accounted as nothing,

But He does according to His will in the host of heaven

And among the inhabitants of earth;

And no one can ward off His hand

Or say to Him, 'What hast Thou done?'"

Now list on pages 100-103 everything you learn about God from marking this passage. (The extra space is so you can add other observations as you do each day's assignments.)

When I speak of God's *sovereignty,* I am referring to the fact that God rules over all. He is totally, supremely, and preeminently over all His creation. Nothing escapes His sovereign control. No one eludes His sovereign plan. Let me diagram these crucial verses for you.

Daniel 4 states that God rules over "the host of heaven." What does this host, or army, include? (See diagram.) There are hosts of good angels who do the bidding of God, and there are hosts of fallen angels who do

the bidding of Satan. In the diagram on page 79, I have placed Satan between the good and the evil angels. Ephesians 2:2 calls him "the prince of the power of the air," the spirit who works in the sons of disobedience. His realm of authority is not only over fallen angels, but also over those who do not know the Lord Jesus Christ, who are "by nature children of wrath" (Ephesians 2:3).

At this point a very legitimate question may arise in your mind: *If God is sovereign and in control over everything, where does that leave the free will of man?*

That's an excellent question, and one that has been debated for centuries. The truth is, God's sovereignty in no way negates the free will of man...nor does man's free will rule out the sovereignty of God!

"But—how could that be?" you ask. "How could both be true? Don't those statements contradict one another?"

To our finite human minds, these twin truths do seem contradictory. If we tried in our wisdom to put them together, we might blow our circuit breakers! That's why we must always remember one overarching fact: *God is incomprehensible.* Because God is God, He is beyond our finite understanding. His ways, His character, and His acts are infinitely beyond our own. We can only understand Him to the depth that He chooses to reveal Himself to us.

God's Word does not reveal to us how His sovereignty and our free will fit together. It simply declares that they do and calls us to place our trust in Him. Remember how He expressed it to the prophet Isaiah? (Once again mark every reference to God with a △ Then add what you learn to your list on pages 100-103.)

◗ ISAIAH 55:8-9

8 "For My thoughts are not your thoughts,

Neither are your ways My ways," declares the LORD.

9 "For as the heavens are higher than the earth,

So are My ways higher than your ways,

And My thoughts than your thoughts."

Faith steps into the picture at this very point. Because we are finite human beings with limited understanding, we must not try to force God's truth to fit into our patterns of thinking. We must simply accept what He says, whether we understand it or not. What He *has* revealed is more than enough to teach us how to live. Beyond that we must say with Paul,

▶ ROMANS 11:33-36

33 Oh, the depth of the riches both of the wisdom and knowledge of God! How unsearchable are His judgments and unfathomable His ways!

34 For WHO HAS KNOWN THE MIND OF THE LORD, OR WHO BECAME HIS COUNSELOR?

35 Or WHO HAS FIRST GIVEN TO HIM THAT IT MIGHT BE PAID BACK TO HIM AGAIN?

36 For from Him and through Him and to Him are all things. To Him be the glory forever. Amen.

(Now go back and once again mark every reference to God, and then add what you learn to your list on pages 100-103.)

What's the bottom line? God is sovereign and in absolute control.

Once we understand and accept the fact that God's sovereignty leaves our free will intact, we must also admit *accountability* to Him for our actions. Matthew 18:7 demonstrates this clearly:

Woe to the world because of its stumbling blocks! For it is inevitable that stumbling blocks come; but woe to that man through whom the stumbling block comes!

Stumbling blocks can only be permitted by a sovereign God. Yet God tells us we are fully accountable if we *cause* these stumbling blocks. We see this same pattern of sovereignty and accountability when Jesus says to Pilate, "You would have no authority over Me, unless it had been given you from above; for this reason he who delivered Me up to you has the greater sin" (John 19:11). God knew all along that Judas Iscariot was going to betray Jesus. Jesus knew it also. God used it to accomplish His plan of redemption, and yet Judas was fully accountable before God!

Reflecting on these things, you might well say, "Kay, it just doesn't seem fair! It doesn't fit. It doesn't seem right. It's hard for me to believe." I understand, but I have to tell you that those kinds of statements are a reflection of biblical immaturity. You are uttering the cries of one who still dines on milk and has not yet tried chewing a sirloin steak! Let's press on to know our God, and then we will never say that anything He does is unfair. Why? Because unfairness is contrary to His character. God is just.

What is your prayer today? Do you need wisdom, revelation, understanding? Are you already craving that submissive spirit of meekness that bows to His mighty sovereignty?

Cry, Beloved. Cry out to your God. He never turns a deaf ear to those who hunger and thirst after righteousness.

— D A Y   T W O —

The LORD of hosts has sworn saying, "Surely, just as I have intended so it has happened, and just as I have planned so it will stand.... For the LORD of hosts has planned, and who can frustrate it? And as for His stretched-out hand, who can turn it back?" (Isaiah 14:24,27)

Let me ask a question of the married people working through this study. Have you ever looked at your mate and wondered if you married the wrong person? Be honest now! I think the majority of us would say yes. I would have to say yes—and I'm sure my husband would say the same!

Such thoughts can be troubling, can't they? Perhaps even panicky. Could you have somehow missed the will of God?

Or possibly you are single, and your friend excitedly introduces you to his or her "intended." You find yourself thinking, *Oh God, this person seems tailor-made for ME, not for my friend! Why didn't I get there first? Was this the one You meant for me?*

As a single person, have you run hither and yon, trying so hard to be at the "right" place at the "right" time so that you might cross paths with the mate of your dreams? Have you traveled from church to church, surveying the prospects, then absolutely panicked for fear you're somehow going to miss God's best?

Thoughts like these can unleash sheer mental torture. Live with these thoughts long enough, and your mind may become paralyzed, spinning you into depression and despair. Yet what you may not realize is that this is a missile from the enemy's arsenal—a destructive tactic as old as the Garden of Eden.

He will try to make you question God's goodness. Question God's timing. Question God's care and concern for you. Question God's control of life's tiny, yet momentous details.

Run to the sovereignty of God, Beloved! Rest in His loving control of every particular of your life.

Perhaps you find yourself attracted to someone else's spouse, and you hear an insistent voice saying, "God's holding back on you. God's keeping you from something you really need. Surely you're an exception to the old rules. How could this be adultery or fornication? This attraction must be from God. It's so pure, it's so lovely. Why, it's even drawn you closer to God! Reach out and take it. Indulge yourself."

Oh, please don't!

Run to the sovereignty of God. Know that, as Isaiah 14:24,27 says, "just as [He has] intended so it has happened, and just as [He has] planned so it will stand.... For the LORD of hosts has planned, and who can frustrate it? And as for His stretched-out hand, who can turn it back?" If you are married, the will of God is your mate—nothing else, no one else.

"But I'm not happy!" you say. "I'm not fulfilled! I've missed what I've always wanted!"

O Beloved, you may have missed what you wanted, but life isn't over. This is temporal—eternity is coming.

Meekness bows the knee and realizes that everything is permitted and used by God for our chastening, our purifying. Meekness says, "Not my will, but Yours be done." Meekness bows before the throne and realizes that the God who sits upon that throne is an all-wise God.

God makes His wise plans on the basis of His righteous character. He has righteous ends in mind and chooses righteous means to achieve those ends.

Meekness knows that the God who sits upon the throne of the universe is a good God.

He delights to bless.

He takes holy pleasure in the ultimate welfare and happiness of His people.

He is kind, benevolent, and full of good will.

Therefore, if you are experiencing neither happiness nor fulfillment in your marriage, or any other relationship, and you have done all you should have in light of His Word, rest! God will see to it that even your heartbreak will work together for good. So bow your knee and say, "I will give Thee thanks forever, because Thou hast done it, and I will wait on Thy name, for it is good" (Psalm 52:9). Because He is God, He will satisfy your thirsty soul. He will fill your hungry soul with what is good (Psalm 107:9).

So many books, tapes, and seminars on marriage have flooded the

Christian marketplace. You would think that the chief end of man (and woman!) is to be happily married! I can't buy that. I must agree with the Westminster Confession that the chief aim of man is "to glorify God and to enjoy Him forever."

Despite all the seminars, the "Encounters," the seemingly endless "biblical formulas," and the detailed marriage manuals that chart all the hows, whys, and wherefores—some men and women still live in their own little hell. They've followed all the counsel, walked through all the steps, and done all they've been told to do, yet nothing has worked.

If your spouse neither cares nor cooperates, what will you do? Will you break God's holy covenant? Will you get a divorce? Will you say, "Surely God doesn't expect me to endure this, to be miserable for the rest of my life"? Or will you in meekness bow the knee and say, "As the Lord has planned, so it has come to pass. If it seems good to You, my Father, it seems good to me. Now Father, perfect that which concerns me. Work it all to Your glory and to my good."

Is God speaking to you through these words, Beloved? I pray that you will listen and that you will not resist His voice.

Your assignment for today is to write down what you have learned about your God.

— D A Y   T H R E E —

If God is a sovereign God, how do you explain the injustices, the holocausts, the rapes, the incest, the abuses, the murders? How do you explain suffering, pain, and terrible cruelty?

I will never forget the night I sat on my bed and read a murderer's detailed description of how he kidnapped, sexually assaulted, and murdered a precious little girl. As he sought to violate her in the backseat of a car, she looked into his eyes and said, "God doesn't like what you're doing. It's wrong."

It so angered the man that he brutally killed her.

I remember tossing that deposition aside, throwing my head back, and fiercely clamping my eyes shut. But to no avail. Tears coursed down my cheeks. "Father," I sobbed, "I don't understand. I just don't understand."

How could God be a God of love and let these things happen?

I think most of us, at one time or another, have struggled with this. How could a sovereign God permit such savagery? How could a loving God allow such beauty and innocence to be desecrated and destroyed by perverted lust?

I had to cling to His Word that night with all my strength. I had to come back again and again to what I know to be true about Him.

His Word tells me that He is sovereign.

His Word tells me that He is love. It is the very essence of His being.

His Word tells me that He is all-seeing and all-knowing. He knows every sparrow that falls from the sky. He had numbered every hair on that little girl's head.

His Word tells me that His children will never be tested beyond that which they can bear and that with the testing will come a way of escape.

His Word tells me that He is just and that one day there will be a strict accounting for the evil committed in our world.

I found comfort that night by clinging to the attributes of God. He is a God of truth, and His very nature demands that He be faithful and true to His promises. Somehow in some way I knew that this little girl had been given the grace of God to bear the perversion and violence of that evil man.

But didn't she lose her life? No, not even that. The Bible says that Jesus is the resurrection and the life. Those who believe in Him shall never die. Her life was not taken from her; she simply stepped from life into Life. And she stepped into our Lord's waiting arms.

Take time to ponder the passages printed out below. As you do, again mark every reference to God with a △ and add what you learn to the list you began on pages 100-103.

▶ DEUTERONOMY 32:39

"See now that I, I am He,

And there is no god besides Me;

It is I who put to death and give life.

I have wounded, and it is I who heal;

And there is no one who can deliver from My hand."

▶ REVELATION 1:17-18

[17] "Do not be afraid; I am the first and the last,

[18] and the living One; and I was dead, and behold, I am alive forevermore, and I have the keys of death and of Hades."

Now take a few minutes and review what you've learned so far this week about God's character and His sovereignty. Use the space below to record your thoughts. If you find yourself struggling with these truths, talk to God about it. Tell Him where you feel confused or unsettled. He knows it anyway, but He wants to hear it from your lips. He loves you!

– D A Y   F O U R –

As we saw yesterday, one of the things that makes it difficult to accept God's sovereignty is the fact that He apparently permits adversity or evil.

And it's true. He *does* permit evil in our world.

Here is what the Scripture says. As you read it, again mark every reference to God with a △. Then list your observations on pages 100-103.

▶ ISAIAH 45:5-7

5 I am the LORD, and there is no other;

Besides Me there is no God.

6 …from the rising to the setting of the sun

…there is no one besides Me.

I am the LORD, and there is no other,

7 The One forming light and creating darkness,

Causing well-being and creating calamity;

I am the LORD who does all these.

▶ ECCLESIASTES 7:13-14

13 Consider the work of God,

For who is able to straighten what He has bent?

14 In the day of prosperity be happy,

But in the day of adversity consider—

God has made the one as well as the other

So that man may not discover anything that will be after him.

One reason we have problems with God's sovereignty in the face of adversity, evil, or calamity is that we are temporal beings. Our vision is temporal, *and we cannot see beyond the limits of our vision.*

I enjoyed twenty-twenty vision right up into my late forties. Yet gradually, as I grew older, I experienced more and more difficulty focusing on things up close to me. It became a bit of a struggle to read a magazine, follow a recipe, or thread a needle. How frustrated I used to get over my blurry vision! But after I received my contact lenses, I gained an entirely new perspective!

This is the way it is with many of us. We are so focused on the future that we can't understand the things happening to us now. Our circumstances seem confusing and don't appear to be taking us in the direction we want to go. Our immediate relationships and situations seem strangely out of focus and confused. We struggle and strain to see more clearly.

This is why some people have problems with the sovereignty of God. They look at the future, imagining they see it clearly. Because of their cherished goals and high expectations, they have difficulty accepting and handling hurts, setbacks, and adversities in daily life. Life seems out of control. How could these bumps and bruises possibly be coming from God?

What they need are spiritual contact lenses. What they need is a proper perspective on the present in light of the *eternal.* Only faith will do. This eternal God who creates prosperity and adversity has neither beginning nor end. He is not confined to the finiteness of time nor to man's reckoning of time. He is never early, never late, and never in a hurry. And whether we understand our immediate circumstances or not, He views our whole earthly pilgrimage through the eyes of eternity. He knows where we are going. He knows how it all fits together. He knows how to extract maximum good and maximum glory out of every situation, *no matter what!*

Meekness then, when faced with adversity, bows the knee. Meekness acknowledges that God is eternal. It says with David, "But as for me, I trust in Thee, O LORD, I say, 'Thou art my God.' My times are in Thy hand" (Psalm 31:14-15).

Meekness looks "not at the things which are seen, but at the things which are not seen; for the things which are seen are temporal, but the things which are not seen are eternal" (2 Corinthians 4:18).

Meekness remembers that it is finite and that God is infinite. The realm of God has no limits or bounds whatsoever.

"But Kay," you say, "it still doesn't seem *fair* for God to let these things happen. Look at all the murderers running around free. Look at all the Christians who love God and are locked up in prisons and labor camps and psychiatric institutions. How could a just, sovereign God allow a Hitler to carry out his holocaust…or let the Chinese crucify, behead, and mutilate millions? How could a just and holy God let Idi Amin live unpunished in a quiet resort after he and his men barbarically dismembered their enemies before the very eyes of their loved ones? How can a merciful God allow countless numbers of little boys and girls to be molested and their assailants go undetected? How? It's not fair! There's nothing right about it!"

When you want to cry out, "It's not fair," you need to go back again to the character of God. God is righteous. He is always good. It's essential to His character that He be so. His actions are always consistent with His character, which is love. The God who sits on His throne can never divest Himself of His love or His righteousness or His holiness or His justice. He cannot take off any one of His attributes and lay it aside and act independently of it. It is part of His being to be just. In all of His actions, God acts with fairness. If He did less, He would no longer be God! Whether He deals with man, angels, or demons, He acts in total equity by rewarding righteousness and punishing sin. And since He knows all, every decree is absolutely just.

Please don't think I'm saying that God decrees or orders men to do evil. This would be contrary to His nature. Remember the warning of James? "Let no one say when he is tempted, 'I am being tempted by God'; for God cannot be tempted by evil, and He Himself does not tempt anyone" (James 1:13).

Those who want everything set down in some logical, five-step presentation (complete with graphs and pie charts) will always struggle with these divine mysteries. This is where meekness and faith come in! Faith says, "God, I don't understand, but I know You are sovereign, loving, and just. I may *never* understand in this life, but I will not accuse You, slander You, nor alter a single one of Your words to fit my poor, limited perspective."

Consider for a moment the life of Moses. He had given God forty years of consecrated obedience through some of the most devastating circumstances you can imagine. Then, in one moment of pressure, he broke. He rashly struck the rock with his staff a second time when God had clearly told him to *speak* to the rock. In so doing, Moses failed to sanctify God in the eyes of His people. So God, in His justice, told Moses that he could never enter the Promised Land. He would see that land of Canaan from the crown of Mount Nebo, but he would never enter it.

And what did Moses say after God pronounced this judgment upon him? Never taking his eyes off God, he said:

> For I proclaim the name of the LORD;
> Ascribe greatness to our God!
> The Rock! His work is perfect,
> For all His ways are just;
> A God of faithfulness and without injustice,
> Righteous and upright is He.
> (Deuteronomy 32:3-4)

O Beloved, meekness does not accuse God of being unrighteous or unjust. Meekness realizes that God is *holy.* He is a morally excellent, perfect being, pure in every aspect. So meekness makes itself low before His might and majesty. Meekness whispers through its tears, "God, I trust You. I know You are holy. I know You are righteous. I know You are just. I accept everything that comes into my life without murmuring, without disputing, without retaliation. I know, God, that You are a God of wrath. I know that within You is a holy hatred for all that is unrighteous—an unquenchable desire to punish all unrighteousness. I know, God, that whatever is inconsistent with You must ultimately be consumed. And I wait for that day when You, in righteousness and justice, will move with wrath."

> For after all it is only just for God to repay with affliction those who afflict you, and to give relief to you who are afflicted and to us as well when the Lord Jesus shall be revealed from heaven with His mighty angels in flaming fire, dealing out retribution to those who do not know God and to those who do not obey the gospel of our Lord Jesus. And these will pay the penalty of eternal destruction, away from the presence of the Lord and from the glory of His power. (2 Thessalonians 1:6-9)

But why does God wait so long?

Why does He let unrighteous men live?

Why does He let mockers go on mocking and scoffers go on scoffing?

Why isn't His judgment swift?

Because, Beloved, God is *merciful and long-suffering*. God is an actively compassionate being. He shows compassion toward those who oppose Him and pursue their own paths. He is slow to anger against those who fail to listen to His warnings or to obey His instructions. The eternal longing for the highest good for His creatures holds back His holy justice. As the old fisherman (who had tasted the patience of his Lord) wrote, "The Lord is not slow about His promise, as some count slowness, but is patient toward you, not wishing for any to perish but for all to come to repentance" (2 Peter 3:9).

There's another question in your heart, isn't there?

If God is not willing that any should perish, what about the heathen? Why are the heathen, who have never heard about God, going to perish? How can God be fair and just and let men go to hell who have never heard about Jesus Christ?

Can we wait until tomorrow to tackle that question? I think that we've had enough for today, don't you? Stop once again and meditate upon all that you have learned today about the sovereignty and character of God. Use the space below to record your thoughts. (The passages of Scripture you read are so good they bear marking, so put your △ in the appropriate places and add what you learn to your list on pages 100-103.)

– D A Y   F I V E –

What about those who have never heard the gospel?

If God is not willing that any should perish, then how could He condemn men and women who die in darkness and spiritual ignorance?

I will never forget talking to a young man who was weeping over the sudden death of a coworker. He was crushed, not only with grief but with guilt. "Because of me," he said, "that man is in hell today! I did not witness to him."

Was that true?

Was there a man in hell because a young friend had failed to witness to him?

If so, where does that leave the sovereignty of God and the eternal destiny of man?

The young man was right about a couple of things. We *are* accountable before the Lord. We *are* our brothers' keepers. We *are* to give the gospel to others so we can say with Paul, "I am innocent of the blood of all men" (Acts 20:26). At the same time, however, *no one's spiritual destiny rests on one individual's faithfulness or unfaithfulness.*

It is the same for those who live their whole lives in spiritual darkness and have never heard the name of Jesus Christ.

The God who sits upon the sovereign throne of all the universe is *self-sufficient.* Within Himself, God is able to act and to bring about His will without any assistance. Although He may use assistance, it is because He chooses to, not out of need. God can and has revealed Himself without any human instrument.

The story of Samuel Morris illustrates this point.

Samuel Morris—or Kaboo, as he was named at birth—was the eldest son of a chieftain of West Africa. And he knew absolutely nothing about God.

In those regions it was the custom for a chief who was defeated in war to give his eldest son as a pawn or hostage to ensure the payment of war indemnity. If payment lagged, he was often subject to torture. Such was the fate of Kaboo.[2]

When he was fifteen, Kaboo became a pawn of war for the third time—only this time his father was unable to pay off his war debts. Furious, the captor began to savagely whip young Kaboo with a stout vine.

The flesh of his back hung in shreds. Soon he became so exhausted from loss of blood and the fever induced by the poison vine that he could no longer stand or even sit up. A cross-tree was then erected and he was carried out and thrown over it while he was again beaten over his raw back.

THE MIRACULOUS ESCAPE

Kaboo hoped that death would release him before he met the awful fate of an unredeemed pawn. A number of Kaboo's tribesmen had been taken as ordinary slaves by this brutal chief. Several of them had been accused as bewitchers. Kaboo had seen them literally torn to pieces by drunken and frenzied men. But he was now faced by an even more diabolical fate.

Already, they had dug a pit in anticipation of the possible failure of his father to return. If his final beating induced no further payment, he was to be buried up to the neck. His mouth would then be propped open, and smeared with a sweet mixture to attract the ants from a nearby anthill. The resulting torment would merely prepare for the final act when another type of insect—the dreaded driver ants—would be permitted to devour his living flesh bit by bit. After the ants had cleaned his bones of every particle of flesh, his white skeleton would then be placed in front of his execution hut as a gentle reminder to all future debtors.

As Kaboo was flung upon the cross-tree for his final beating, all hope as well as physical strength left him. He longed only for the boon of death.

Then, suddenly something very strange happened. A great light like a flash of lightning broke over him. The light blinded all about him. An audible voice that seemed to come from above commanded him to rise and flee. All heard the voice and saw the light but saw no man.

At the same time there occurred one of those instantaneous healings which science can neither deny nor explain. In the twinkling of an eye Kaboo found his strength restored. He had had nothing to eat or drink all that day. Yet he felt neither hunger nor thirst nor weakness. Leaping up, he obeyed the mysterious voice and fled from the astonished natives with the speed of a deer.

What was the source of the mysterious light that had brought him new strength and freedom? Kaboo did not know or suspect. He had never heard of the Christian God. He knew nothing of special acts of Divine Providence. He had never heard of a Savior who had once been put in pawn, a ransom for many. The earthly prince who had just hung over a cross-tree of torture did not dream of a heavenly Prince who had been mocked and beaten as a prisoner and had suffered a degraded death by slow torture upon a tree.

But Kaboo did know that some strange and invisible power had come to his rescue. At one moment he had been too ill to sit erect and now he was running away at top speed. It was on a Friday that he made his escape. Kaboo never forgot that day. He called it his Deliverance Day, and as long as he lived he always celebrated the day of the week by fasting, taking neither food nor water.[3]

After fleeing from his enemies, Kaboo finally found his way to a coffee plantation.

His Kru companion had been listening to the missionaries and had learned to pray. Kaboo saw him on his knees, both hands lifted up and face upturned. When Kaboo asked him what he was doing, he replied, "I am talking to God."

"Who is your God?" asked Kaboo.

"He is my Father," answered the boy.

"Then you are talking to your Father," said Kaboo. Ever afterward he called praying "talking to my Father." To his childlike faith, prayer was as simple and as sure as conversing with an earthly parent.

The next Sunday Kaboo was invited to attend church. He found a crowd gathered around a woman who was speaking through an interpreter. She was telling them about the conversion of Saul; how a light from heaven suddenly shone upon him and a mysterious voice spoke from above.

Kaboo cried out: "That's just what I saw! I have seen that light! That is the same light that saved me and brought me here!" Kaboo had been wondering all the time why he had been so marvelously saved from death and guided through the forest. Now, in a flash he began to understand.[4]

God cannot save a soul until that soul has knowledge of Him and exercises conscious faith. Yet the Providence of God often spares the lives and heals the bodies of those who are yet strangers to Him, either in answer to the prayers of believers or for His own good purposes.

Perhaps you are saying, "I know that you have told me all this about God, but what if He changes? Don't we see a different God in the New

Testament than we do in the Old Testament? In the Old Testament He required Joshua to put to death all the inhabitants of Jericho. But in the New Testament He won't even allow the scribes and the Pharisees to stone a woman caught in the act of adultery. So...what if He changes again?"

God has not changed, Beloved. He *cannot* change. In theological terms He is "immutable." God is always the same in His nature, His character, and His will. Malachi 3:6 says, "For I, the LORD, do not change." Hebrews 13:8 says, "Jesus Christ is the same yesterday and today, yes and forever."

There are not two Gods—a God of the Old Testament and a God of the New Testament. Jesus is not a kinder, gentler version of the Old Testament's Jehovah. Mercy and long-suffering have always been attributes of God. When He slaughtered the children and adults of Jericho, He was acting in His just wrath, for they had had years to repent and did not. The children of Israel could not have even taken possession of Canaan until the iniquity of the Amorites was "full." This is what God told Abraham in Genesis 15:16.

Here is one more "What if...?"—and a frightening one. "What if God ceases to be? What if science somehow proves that God does not exist?"

Humankind will always try to prove God does not exist. People will argue with you and come at you from a thousand different angles. But you can know that God is *self-existent.* There is nothing upon which God depends for His existence except Himself. The whole basis of His existence is within Himself. There was a time when nothing existed but God alone. He added nothing to Himself by Creation.

Man will never blot out the knowledge of God from the face of this earth. He is the great I AM. "I AM WHO I AM.... This is My name forever, and this is My memorial-name to all generations" (Exodus 3:14-15).

When confronted with all this, some would still say God is not sovereign. So, let's suppose for a minute that God is not. Who then *is* in control?

Man?

The devil?

Blind fate?

If man is in control, then he would have to be as great and powerful as God Himself. He would have to be capable of usurping the will of God and doing whatever he wants to do. Would you accept a teaching like this?

If Satan is in control, then he can do whatever he wishes without God's permission. He can harm whomever he wants and meddle in any and all of God's plans. If this is so, then Satan is as powerful as God. Could that be? Could a created being actually set his throne above the Creator? No. He tried and found himself condemned to the lake of fire (Isaiah 14:12-15).

But then, if neither man nor the devil is in control, are we in the hands of fate? If that's so, then some power or force, whatever it may be, is determining our destiny rather than God. God is not transcendent; He is not above His creation but has been usurped from His sovereign throne by that which He brought into being.

And—reason with me—if God is not sovereign, how can He tell us "in everything give thanks; for this is God's will for you in Christ Jesus" (1 Thessalonians 5:18) and then promise us that all things will work together for good and be used to conform us to the character of our Lord Jesus Christ (Romans 8:28-30)?

What are the alternatives to a sovereign, all-powerful God? There aren't any, are there?

Meekness rests its childlike trust in the Lord and says, "My Lord and my God, if it pleases You, it pleases me."

Listen to the way David expressed his heart to the Lord, Beloved. Listen to the voice of meekness in the face of sovereignty.

O LORD, my heart is not proud, nor my eyes haughty;

Nor do I involve myself in great matters,

Or in things too difficult for me.
Surely I have composed and quieted my soul;
Like a weaned child rests against his mother,
My soul is like a weaned child within me.
O Israel, hope in the LORD
From this time forth and forever.
(Psalm 131)

On this final day on the character and sovereignty of God, I urge you to rehearse what you have observed and recorded about God this week. Read and meditate on the list you've made. Ask God to work into your heart the things that you have taken into your mind.[5] In fervent prayer, submit your will to His.

I can't begin to describe the harvest of peace you will reap.

WHAT I OBSERVED ABOUT GOD FROM THE WORD

WHAT I OBSERVED ABOUT GOD FROM THE WORD

WHAT I OBSERVED ABOUT GOD FROM THE WORD

WHAT I OBSERVED ABOUT GOD FROM THE WORD

MEMORY VERSE

Blessed are the gentle, for they shall inherit the earth.

MATTHEW 5:5

SMALL-GROUP DISCUSSION QUESTIONS

1. How would you explain the sovereignty of God?
   a. Define sovereignty.
   b. Over what things is God sovereign?
   c. Is God's sovereignty a concept we can fully grasp? Why or why not?
2. How does knowing the character of God help you to understand His sovereignty?
3. What did you learn about the attributes of God? How would you define them? What practical implications do they have for your life?
4. How do sovereignty and the character of God relate to meekness?
5. Have the class recite Matthew 5:5.
6. How would you define meekness? In what ways does your definition of meekness differ from the world's definition?
7. If God is not sovereign, what then?
8. Do you trust God's character and His love for you? If not, what will it take for you to make the decision to trust Him?
9. How has God spoken to you this week? Is there anything you are struggling with?
10. Close with a prayer for one another.

MEEKNESS: IS IT WEAKNESS OR STRENGTH?

— D A Y   O N E —

How relieved I was when someone recognized us and ushered us through the crowd.

When we first stepped through the door of the funeral parlor, all I could see was wall-to-wall people. I wondered how we would ever get to Bobby and Diane without pushing our way past people who'd been waiting for three hours to express their love and condolences to the family.

Just seven months before, we had driven to Mobile, Alabama, for Scott and Christy's wedding. Now we were in Mobile again—unexpectedly—for Scott's funeral. All we wanted was to be at the side of the couple who had meant so much to us through the years—and now faced one of life's most heart-searing trials.

Two days earlier I had received a message at Precept Ministries International to call Bobby at home immediately. Bobby had just received word that his older son, Scott, had been killed in an automobile accident—an accident due to the negligence of another person. In a matter of minutes the life of a very godly and talented young man was unexpectedly snuffed out; the light was gone. Suddenly it didn't seem right for the sun to continue shining that day, for the birds to continue singing, or for people to be walking and talking and laughing on the sidewalks outside. The sting of death had caused our hearts to swell until we thought they would burst from sorrow.

As Jack and I were ushered into the room where a coffin housed Scott's now vacant human tent, my eye caught Bobby's as he motioned us to himself. In a moment, our arms were around each other. Then he gently pushed me back.

"I'm all right, Kay," he said. "God has met with me. Everything I have learned from studying the Word of God has held me and prepared me for this moment. His Word is true. God is good, and He is sovereign."

In that moment, I stood face to face with true meekness.

A few moments later, I heard similar words from Diane as Jack and I embraced her. The same confidence. The same peace. The same trust. The same meekness.

As I write these words, it has been a little over a year and a half since Scott's homegoing. Jack and I have talked, prayed, and cried together with Bobby and Diane. Yet I have never seen them waver from the certainty that God operated according to His plans for Scott. It was God who had knit Scott together in Diane's womb, and it was God who had numbered Scott's days…when as yet there were none.

I have seen meekness in motion for the past eighteen months—lived out for all to see in the most difficult and heart wrenching of circumstances, the death of a child. And knowing Scott as we did, we are confident that if he could speak a word to us from heaven, he would model the same steady, godly meekness. It is a meekness which one day will inherit the earth, when the King of kings will sit on his glorious throne and rule the world in righteousness and truth.

Just before he died, Scott had spoken of his willingness to give his life for the salvation of his loved ones, his family and friends. Someday—in all probability sooner than we think—these meek people will inherit the earth.

This week we will continue to explore the subject of meekness—a beautiful jewel of eternal truth which I pray will adorn your life and mine.

It is an elegant gem with many facets, enhanced as we examine it from different angles and it catches the brilliant light of God's truth. Truly it is a jewel fit for our Lord's crown.

Meekness, translated *gentle* by the NASB in Matthew 5:5, was one of the great words of Greek ethics. The Greek word *praotes* refers to an inward grace of the soul. It is what I saw in Bobby and Diane—an acceptance of God's dealings with us as good. Good because they draw us closer to Him. Good because we know we can trust God and rest in His sovereignty even though the situation itself does not seem good.

Meekness implies submission to God. Not a passive submission that shrugs its shoulders and says, "Oh well, I can't do anything about it anyway," but an active submission, a choosing to accept God's ways without murmuring or disputing. Meekness is neither weakness nor complacency.

Aristotle defined meekness with great care. He described it as the mean between excessive anger and the inability to show anger at all. Therefore, a meek individual is one who is angry on the right occasion with the right people at the right moment for the right length of time.

Dr. John MacArthur has described meekness as "anger under control." But what kind of anger? Because meekness is never self-centered, the anger is not about that which happens to me but rather a righteous anger at what is wrongly done to others.

Perhaps you have been taught that all anger is sin. Yet what does Scripture say? Listen to Ephesians 4:26-27:

> BE ANGRY, AND yet DO NOT SIN; do not let the sun go down on your anger, and do not give the devil an opportunity.

What does this verse teach us about anger? Is it sin? Explain why you answer as you do. It will help cement the truth in your mind.

The Greek term for *meekness* has its roots in the domestication of animals. Today we talk about a horse that has been "broken," meaning that the animal has learned to accept control by its master and is properly behaved. From there, the term has been extended to include *people* who are properly behaved. The meek are those of gentle behavior, loving and submissive.

But it is in the Word of God that the gem of meekness is cut, polished, and shot through with inner fire. As we have learned already, meekness accepts all of God's ways with us as good and therefore does not murmur or dispute.

Psalm 37:1-11 shows us how meekness responds when it's "under fire." Read the passage through carefully, and mark the phrases "do not fret" and "inherit the land," each in a distinctive way. Also look for the word "humble" (the same word translated "meek") and underline what God says will happen to the humble.

◐ PSALM 37:1-11

1 Do not fret because of evildoers,

   Be not envious toward wrongdoers.

2 For they will wither quickly like the grass,

   And fade like the green herb.

3 Trust in the LORD, and do good;

   Dwell in the land and cultivate faithfulness.

4 Delight yourself in the LORD;

   And He will give you the desires of your heart.

5 Commit your way to the LORD,

   Trust also in Him, and He will do it.

6 And He will bring forth your righteousness as the light,

And your judgment as the noonday.

7 Rest in the LORD and wait patiently for Him;

Do not fret because of him who prospers in his way,

Because of the man who carries out wicked schemes.

8 Cease from anger, and forsake wrath;

Do not fret, it leads only to evildoing.

9 For evildoers will be cut off,

But those who wait for the LORD, they will inherit the land.

10 Yet a little while and the wicked man will be no more;

And you will look carefully for his place, and he will not be there.

11 But the humble will inherit the land,

And will delight themselves in abundant prosperity.

We also see in this passage four specific responses of "grace under fire."

Meekness trusts (verses 3-4). Trust is a facet of meekness because meekness trusts in the Lord, delighting in Him.

Meekness commits (verse 5). Because of its steady trust, meekness can commit its way to the Lord.

Meekness rests and waits (verses 6-8). Meekness rests in Him, waiting patiently for whatever is God's pleasure. It does not fret and stew over the apparent prosperity of the wicked but focuses all its energies into waiting upon the Lord.

Meekness is confident (verses 9,11). Meekness knows that no matter how desperate the situation may appear, in the long run it will gain a glorious inheritance in the Lord.

To put it in a single phrase, meekness is humble submission to the will of the Father.

Do you remember how Joseph loved and accepted his brothers—the very brothers who had plotted his death, then sold him into slavery? Meekness caused Joseph to look beyond the cruel actions of his brothers to the sovereignty of God. And he was ready to accept *all* of God's dealings with him without bitterness. Do you remember what he said to his brothers when they were trembling with justifiable fear? Joseph was in a place of supreme power. Their lives were literally in his hands! Yet what did he tell them?

> Do not be afraid, for am I in God's place? And as for you, you meant evil against me, but God meant it for good in order to bring about this present result, to preserve many people alive. (Genesis 50:19-20)

Now that's power under control! Those are the words of a powerful man and yet a man who was meek before the Lord.

Meekness is walking under the control of the Holy Spirit, "always giving thanks for all things in the name of our Lord Jesus Christ to God, even the Father" (Ephesians 5:20).

Meekness manifests itself in its reaction to evil—by turning the other cheek, loving its enemies, and praying for those who persecute it (Matthew 5:39,44). Meekness can do this because it realizes that the insults and injuries which evil men and women may inflict are permitted by God and will be used by Him to purify and build godly character.

Meekness is not weakness but incredible power under the control and guidance of God Himself.

Where does meekness come from? It's actually part of our inheritance as children of God. As we shall see later, it is a fruit of God's indwelling Holy Spirit. It is birthed in poverty of spirit when we see that in ourselves—

we are nothing,
> we have nothing,
>> and we can do nothing
>>> to please God.

When we finally comprehend what an impossible mess we have made of our lives, what else can we do but submit in meekness to God's sovereignty and cast ourselves upon El Shaddai, the All-Sufficient One? Apart from Him there really is no life!

Spend some time, Beloved, in prayer. Review what you have learned about meekness. In the space that follows, list some of the ways meekness behaves. Ask God to show you where you are lacking in meekness. Then commit your way to Him, trust in Him, and He will bring it to pass.

You have His Word on it!

– D A Y   T W O –

If you are confused or maybe even troubled about how meekness is lived out in a person's life, you need only look at the person and life of our Lord Jesus Christ. In Him we see the highest and most accurate demonstration of meekness.

Read the words of our Lord recorded in Matthew 11:28-30, and watch for the word *meek*. When you find it, underline it.

Come to Me, all who are weary and heavy-laden, and I will give you rest. Take My yoke upon you, and learn from Me, for I am gentle [meek] and humble in heart; and YOU SHALL FIND REST FOR YOUR SOULS. For My yoke is easy, and My load is light.

According to these verses:

1. How does Jesus describe Himself?

2. What are the various things He tells us to do in this passage? List them below.

3. What will Jesus give us? Are there any conditions?

A yoke was a wooden frame that was put on the backs of animals and around their necks. It joined two or more animals for a common task, such as plowing or pulling a load.

4. What do you learn from Matthew 11:28-30 about being joined or yoked with Jesus Christ?

5. If you were yoked with Jesus Christ, who do you think would "pull the load," and according to these verses, what would this arrangement bring to you?

Now then, let's take a closer look at our Lord, who is meek and humble in heart, and see what we can learn for our own lives.

We said that meekness was used to describe domesticated animals who learned to accept their masters' control and who were properly behaved. We saw that it was a submissive, trusting attitude toward God. No one has ever manifested this more than God's own Son. He was the One who said, "My food is to do the will of Him who sent Me, and to accomplish His work" (John 4:34).

In John 8:28-29, we read:

Jesus therefore said, "When you lift up the Son of Man, then you will know that I am He, and I do nothing on My own initiative, but I speak these things as the Father taught Me. And He who sent Me is with Me; He has not left Me alone, for I always do the things that are pleasing to Him."

1. How do these verses demonstrate the meekness of Jesus Christ?

2. What do you learn from this passage that you can apply to your own life?

We also saw that meekness is anger under control. Meekness is not apathy! It is not a milquetoast character, nor a doormat mentality. How does anger under control behave?

Read John 2:13-17 printed out below.

And the Passover of the Jews was at hand, and Jesus went up to Jerusalem. And He found in the temple those who were selling oxen and sheep and doves, and the moneychangers seated. And He made a scourge of cords, and drove them all out of the temple, with the sheep and the oxen; and He poured out the coins of the moneychangers, and overturned their tables; and to those who were selling the doves He said, "Take these things away; stop making My Father's house a house of merchandise." His disciples remembered that it was written, "ZEAL FOR THY HOUSE WILL CONSUME ME."

1. Would it have been meek or apathetic for Jesus to ignore the money-changers? Explain your answer.

2. Was Jesus angry at the right time with the right people and for the right reason? Again, explain your answer from the previous passage.

Finally, before we conclude today's study, come with me to the Garden of Gethsemane. Once again we will see the example of meekness submitting to God's sovereign will—no matter what the cost!

Read the following passage. Mark in a distinctive color or way every pronoun (He, Me, etc.) which refers to Jesus. Then answer the questions that follow.

▶ MATTHEW 26:37-44

37 And He took with Him Peter and the two sons of Zebedee, and began to be grieved and distressed.

38 Then He said to them, "My soul is deeply grieved, to the point of death; remain here and keep watch with Me."

39 And He went a little beyond them, and fell on His face and prayed,

saying, "My Father, if it is possible, let this cup pass from Me; yet not as I will, but as Thou wilt."

40 And He came to the disciples and found them sleeping, and said to Peter, "So, you men could not keep watch with Me for one hour?

41 "Keep watching and praying, that you may not enter into temptation; the spirit is willing, but the flesh is weak."

42 He went away again a second time and prayed, saying, "My Father, if this cannot pass away unless I drink it, Thy will be done."

43 And again He came and found them sleeping, for their eyes were heavy.

44 And He left them again, and went away and prayed a third time, saying the same thing once more.

1. What does Jesus ask of His Father?

2. What is the "cup" He speaks of? Compare this with John 18:11 and write your answer.

3. How many times did Jesus pray this prayer?

4. How does this passage demonstrate the meekness of Jesus?

Beloved, there is our Example! The yoke is waiting. Will you take it and learn from Him? Believe me, it will be the only way you will find rest for your soul in your day-by-day living. Don't be afraid of that yoke! As He has told us, His yoke is easy, and His load is light.

In the space provided below, list everything you have learned so far about meekness—what it is and what it isn't! The review will help anchor these things in your mind.

Now then, you might want to write out a prayer to the Lord as you contemplate His yoke. If you fear it, tell Him so! He will meet you at the very point of your fear. Ask Him to show you His perfect love which casts out all fear (1 John 4:18).

— D A Y   T H R E E —

We have defined *meekness,* and in the Lord Jesus Christ we have seen it clothed in flesh. Now let's consider what meekness looks like as you and I live it out in our daily world.

When God made the earth and put man upon it, He intended for man to rule as His vice-regent over Creation. All man had to do was walk in submission to God, in total dependence upon his Creator. For that submission to be authentic, however, it had to be *voluntary.* So God gave man a free will. He could choose to walk with God, or he could choose to turn his back and walk an independent path.

Would man obey and continue to walk with his Creator? It had to be put to the test. And strangely enough, the test was embodied in a tree. The tree of the knowledge of good and evil.

God's instructions were very clear. "From any tree of the garden you may eat freely; but from the tree of the knowledge of good and evil you shall not eat, for in the day that you eat from it you shall surely die" (Genesis 2:16-17). Man was not blind to the consequences of his sin. God tells us very clearly in 1 Timothy 2:14 that Adam was not deceived. Eve was, but not Adam. He knew exactly what he was doing when he listened to the voice of his wife rather than the voice of God. He ate of the fruit of the tree in willful disobedience. In so doing, Adam chose to walk independently of God and lost the right to rule as God's vice-regent on earth.

Man lost the earth because he was not willing to submit to God. Only meekness will regain that which was lost in the Garden, for "Blessed are the meek, for they shall inherit the earth."

As we have already noted, the starting point of meekness is poverty of spirit. Before we can ever come to salvation, we must demonstrate the meekness that bows to God's authority and lordship over our lives. Jesus makes this plain as He comes to the conclusion of His Sermon on the Mount in Matthew 7:13-23. Those who call Him "Lord" but do not live as His subjects will not enter the kingdom of heaven. To call Him "Lord," and yet fail to do His will, clearly shows that we have never been truly born again.

I have mentioned several times that meekness is part of the fruit of the Holy Spirit. Take a moment to read Galatians 5:22-23, printed out below.

But the fruit of the Spirit is love, joy, peace, patience, kindness, goodness, faithfulness, gentleness [meekness], self-control; against such things there is no law.

How many "fruits" do you see in this passage? Write down the number.

What number did you come up with? The correct answer should be *ONE ninefold fruit.*

Did you notice that the subject and verb are singular? "The fruit...is"! When you are under the control of the Holy Spirit, *all* these things will be manifest in your life. Meekness is a work of God's Spirit in our lives. It can never be generated in our own flesh. If you've ever encountered the artificial, manufactured sort of meekness, you'll remember that it seemed as phony as a yellow, three-dollar bill. Only *God* can make you meek.

Let's look now at James 1:21 and consider a few questions.

Therefore putting aside all filthiness and all that remains of wickedness, in humility receive the word implanted, which is able to save your souls.

1. When James writes "in humility receive the word implanted," the word for *humility* is the same word that is sometimes translated *meekness.* According to this verse, what does meekness have to do with your growth?

2. If I receive God's word in meekness, how will I behave? As you answer this question, remember how we have defined *meekness*.

Now take some time with Psalm 25:9, printed below, and answer the questions which follow. (In the Old Testament the word for *meekness* is often translated *humble* or *afflicted*.)

He leads the humble in justice,
And He teaches the humble His way.

1. According to this verse, whom does the Lord lead and in what way?

2. To whom does He teach His way?

Are you willing to be led? Are you teachable? Are you willing to receive with meekness the engrafted Word of God? When you become more than a "hearer of the Word" and begin to walk in obedience as a "doer of the Word," it will show!

Summarizing what we've learned today, if you are going to be meek, you will submit to God's authority over your life, even as Jesus submitted to the authority of the Father. You will walk carefully, filled with the Spirit. You will be that good soil that receives God's Word and bears fruit.

How does your life measure up to what you have seen today? Think about it. Ponder these things in your heart. Ask God to reveal to you any way in which you have failed to be meek.

— D A Y   F O U R —

How is meekness to be characterized in our dealings with others?

Both Galatians 6:1 and 2 Timothy 2:24-26 use the word *meekness*. Read these passages, and mark or underline the word *meekness*. Then carefully note what you learn about the role of meekness.

❿ GALATIANS 6:1 (KJV)

Brethren, if a man be overtaken in a fault, ye which are spiritual, restore such an one in the spirit of meekness; considering thyself, lest thou also be tempted.

❿ 2 TIMOTHY 2:24-26 (KJV)

24 And the servant of the Lord must not strive; but be gentle unto all men, apt to teach, patient,

25 in meekness instructing those that oppose themselves; if God peradventure will give them repentance to the acknowledging of the truth;

26 and that they may recover themselves out of the snare of the devil, who are taken captive by him at his will.

1. With what similar problem do these two passages deal?

2. What specific thing(s) about meekness have you learned from these two passages?

Whenever I think of correction and how we are to correct one another in meekness, I can't help but remember a night years ago when my husband brought to my attention my lack of gentleness in dealing with people.

It was in the days of "the barn loft" at Precept Ministries International. We launched our ministry with two renovated barns on our Chattanooga property. One was a long, low cow barn, and the second was a two-story barn with a large loft, which we used for our auditorium. Those were precious days, and we all look back on them with fond memories. They were days of growth and maturing...for all of us.

One night the loft was packed with over 250 young people, and I delivered a very strong message, calling them to holiness of life. However, that night as Jack and I crawled into bed, he said to me, "Kay, I didn't hear any love in your voice tonight."

"But those teens know I love them!" I retorted.

"I know," he persisted, "but I still didn't hear any love in your voice."

I didn't say another word. I simply turned to my side of the bed and thought, *What do you know about it, anyway? You don't know how to work with teens.*

I closed my eyes in disgust. Things would look better in the morning.

But sleep wouldn't come.

Jack's voice rang over and over in my mind: *"I didn't hear any love in your voice tonight."*

Finally despairing of sleep, I got up, got out my concordance, and looked up every reference to *gentle*. I will never forget the verse I discovered that night: "Thy gentleness makes me great" (Psalm 18:35). How I wept before God. How I pleaded with Him. *O Father, just bring them back. I know that I don't deserve to teach them again, but please…just bring them back so I can tell them I was so wrong…so I can ask them to forgive me.*

He brought them back. The barn loft was packed again. I stood before them and wept, asking their forgiveness and telling them what God had taught me.

O Beloved, no matter how grievous the sin, no matter how strong the snare of Satan, we are not to correct anyone in any other way except meekness. All our righteous indignation must be brought under the control of meekness. Otherwise, when we seek to restore a brother and recover him out of the snare of the devil, he will never see the character of God and be drawn to Him. Instead, he will be repulsed by our behavior and have a good excuse for excusing himself!

Finally today, let's look at Moses, another example of how meekness behaves in its dealings with others. Read the following passage, and then answer the questions.

● NUMBERS 12:1-13

1 Then Miriam and Aaron spoke against Moses because of the Cushite woman whom he had married (for he had married a Cushite woman);

2 and they said, "Has the LORD indeed spoken only through Moses? Has He not spoken through us as well?" And the LORD heard it.

3 (Now the man Moses was very humble, more than any man who was on the face of the earth.)

4 And suddenly the LORD said to Moses and Aaron and to Miriam, "You three come out to the tent of meeting." So the three of them came out.

5 Then the LORD came down in a pillar of cloud and stood at the doorway of the tent, and He called Aaron and Miriam. When they had both come forward,

6 He said,

"Hear now My words:

If there is a prophet among you,

I, the LORD, shall make Myself known to him in a vision.

I shall speak with him in a dream.

7 "Not so, with My servant Moses,

He is faithful in all My household;

8 With him I speak mouth to mouth,

Even openly, and not in dark sayings,

And he beholds the form of the LORD.

Why then were you not afraid

To speak against My servant, against Moses?"

9 So the anger of the LORD burned against them and He departed.

10 But when the cloud had withdrawn from over the tent, behold, Miriam was leprous, as white as snow. As Aaron turned toward Miriam, behold, she was leprous.

11 Then Aaron said to Moses, "Oh, my lord, I beg you, do not account *this* sin to us, in which we have acted foolishly and in which we have sinned.

12 "Oh, do not let her be like one dead, whose flesh is half eaten away when he comes from his mother's womb!"

13 And Moses cried out to the LORD, saying, "O God, heal her, I pray!"

1. What do you learn about Moses and meekness from this passage?

2. How did Moses respond to Miriam and Aaron when they attacked him?

3. How did God respond?

4. How does Moses manifest meekness in Numbers 12:9-13?

5. Have you ever been unjustly attacked or falsely accused by any member of your family? How did you respond?

Did their unjust attack or accusation cause you to slip into depression? If so, that's a sure sign that you did not respond in meekness! Meekness is neither elated nor cast down because it is not occupied with self at all.[1] Meekness does not get angry at what is done to it, but meekness gets angry at what is wrongly done to others.

We need to look at one more passage from Moses' life. Remember what we learned about Moses, that he "was very humble [meek], more than any man who was on the face of the earth" (Numbers 12:3).

Yet meekness is not weakness. It is power under control. This is clearly seen in Numbers 16:1-4,28-35. The sons of Korah challenged Moses' leadership. They were disobeying and resisting the authority of God, not the authority of Moses. But Moses went to his knees before the Lord. As God's representative, Moses could not yield his God-given leadership and allow the sons of Korah to rebel against God. Therefore, in meekness Moses called down the judgment of God, and the earth opened and consumed the 250 men who were transgressing.

In Numbers 16:41-50 we see another example of meekness not caring to vindicate itself. When the congregation of the sons of Israel grumbled against Moses and Aaron, God was angered and sent a plague in judgment. Moses interceded for the people, even as he interceded for Miriam. Never forget it, meekness is *not* weakness! It is *not* a milquetoast mentality.

Meekness holds its ground when God's honor and glory are at stake.

Meekness does not become a doormat for sin.

Meekness reflects the blinding radiance of God's Son, the Bright Morning Star, in the midst of a perverse, self-seeking generation.

And so, as those who have been chosen of God, holy and beloved, put on a heart of compassion, kindness, humility, gentleness [meekness] and patience; bearing with one another, and forgiving each other, whoever has a complaint against anyone; just as the Lord forgave you, so also should you. (Colossians 3:12-13)

— D A Y   F I V E —

What eats at the gut of your soul, my friend? Is there something corroding the reflection of His beauty in your countenance? What torments you behind those closed doors of your mind? Is it a bitterness of soul that rises up within you at every memory of a specific episode in your life? It can be done away with today if you will listen carefully to God's Spirit as He speaks to you through His Word.

Meekness is a sure cure for bitterness. As a matter of fact, if there is any bitterness in your life, you can be set free *today*.

Or if you aren't troubled with bitterness, I'm sure God could bring across your path someone who *is* bitter…and you will be equipped to share with him or her what you have learned. You and I aren't left here on earth just to be ministered to. We are to become ministers to others, stewards of the mysteries of God. So study well and watch and pray for that bitter, unhappy soul who crosses your path in the near future. When God brings that person into your life, you will be ready—an instrument of healing in the Great Physician's skillful hands.

Carefully and prayerfully read Hebrews 12:1-17 printed below. When you come to the word *bitterness,* underline it or note it in some special way. Ask God to open the eyes of your understanding. Ask Him to speak to your heart in a direct, personal way. (The Holy Spirit loves to answer prayers like these!) While you have your pen, pencil, or marker out, I want you to highlight two other words as well: *endure* or *endurance,* and *discipline.*

❶ HEBREWS 12:1-17

1 Therefore, since we have so great a cloud of witnesses surrounding us, let us also lay aside every encumbrance, and the sin which so easily entangles us, and let us run with endurance the race that is set before us,

2 fixing our eyes on Jesus, the author and perfecter of faith, who for the joy set before Him endured the cross, despising the shame, and has sat down at the right hand of the throne of God.

3 For consider Him who has endured such hostility by sinners against Himself, so that you may not grow weary and lose heart.

4 You have not yet resisted to the point of shedding blood in your striving against sin;

5 and you have forgotten the exhortation which is addressed to you as sons,

"MY SON, DO NOT REGARD LIGHTLY THE DISCIPLINE OF THE

LORD,

NOR FAINT WHEN YOU ARE REPROVED BY HIM;

6 FOR THOSE WHOM THE LORD LOVES HE DISCIPLINES,

AND HE SCOURGES EVERY SON WHOM HE RECEIVES."

7 It is for discipline that you endure; God deals with you as with sons; for what son is there whom his father does not discipline?

8 But if you are without discipline, of which all have become partakers, then you are illegitimate children and not sons.

9 Furthermore, we had earthly fathers to discipline us, and we respected them; shall we not much rather be subject to the Father of spirits, and live?

10 For they disciplined us for a short time as seemed best to them, but He disciplines us for our good, that we may share His holiness.

11 All discipline for the moment seems not to be joyful, but sorrowful; yet to those who have been trained by it, afterwards it yields the peaceful fruit of righteousness.

12 Therefore, strengthen the hands that are weak and the knees that are feeble,

13 and make straight paths for your feet, so that the limb which is lame may not be put out of joint, but rather be healed.

14 Pursue peace with all men, and the sanctification without which no one will see the Lord.

15 See to it that no one comes short of the grace of God; that no root of bitterness springing up causes trouble, and by it many be defiled;

16 that there be no immoral or godless person like Esau, who sold his own birthright for a single meal.

17 For you know that even afterwards, when he desired to inherit the blessing, he was rejected, for he found no place for repentance, though he sought for it with tears.

The theme of this passage is enduring discipline as God's children. This passage warns us against giving up, growing weary, and losing heart.

Why might we fail to endure? Because no discipline for the present time seems pleasant. Therefore, instead of responding to discipline, instead of seeing it as beneficial in our lives so that we might share in His holiness, we are apt to become discouraged. We may allow the discipline of God to wound us and remove us from effective service for Him.

Another danger is the possibility of falling short of the grace of God when He disciplines us. Instead of responding rightly, we allow a poisonous root of bitterness to spring up within us, causing us trouble and defiling others.

Look again at Hebrews 12:15: "See to it that no one comes short of the grace of God; that no root of bitterness springing up causes trouble, and by it many be defiled."

May I ask you a question? How would meekness respond to the discipline of God?

Meekness always responds to God in submission and trust. It does not fight or struggle. It does not contend with God. As we have already said, it realizes that the insults and injuries which others may inflict upon it are filtered through fingers of love, and permitted and used by God for our discipline and growth.

There it is, Beloved! The key to standing strong against bitterness! Bitterness comes when you do not bow in submission before God, when you resist His discipline, when you do not endure and persevere. *Bitterness comes when you fall short of the grace of God.* To endure means to abide under, not to run away. In meekness we can persevere because we see everything as coming from God and, therefore, having a divine purpose. Are you enduring, my friend, or are you running away?

What does it mean to come short of the grace of God? First, let's define *grace.* You have often heard the definition that grace is "unmerited favor," and that's exactly right. Grace is God's favor to those of us who did not merit, earn, or deserve it in any way.

But I've fallen in love with yet another definition of grace: "Grace is all that Christ is, made available to me." Therefore, Beloved, for you to fall short of the grace of God is for you to fail to appropriate all that God has for you!

Romans 5:2 says that when you were saved you obtained an introduction by faith into the grace of God in which you stand. There it is! Everything that you will ever need, made available to you! You are standing in God's adequacy for every situation of life. To fall short then of the grace of God is to fail to appropriate that in which you stand. It's just a matter of stooping down and in faith scooping it up because you stand with all the grace of God surrounding you.

So stoop and scoop!

In 2 Corinthians 12:1-10 Paul tells about a time when the Lord disciplined him after he was given a staggering vision of heaven. Paul saw revelations that were so celestial and magnificent that God was concerned for His servant. He didn't want the visions to become stumbling blocks to Paul. He didn't want Paul to become puffed up with pride or self-importance. As a result, God gave Paul "a thorn in the flesh," a messenger of Satan to torment him.

Whatever that "thorn" was, it was *very* painful and distressing. Paul went to the Lord three times, pleading with Him to take it away. What was God's answer?

And He has said to me, "My grace is sufficient for you, for power is perfected in weakness." (2 Corinthians 12:9)

The phrasing of the Lord's answer to Paul is significant. The Greek verb translated here as "He has said" is in the perfect tense. Seeing that, we gain a clearer picture of God's reply to His distressed servant. God was saying to him, "Don't ask Me again to remove this thorn in the flesh. *This is My answer and it stands.* My grace is sufficient for you, Paul, for power is perfected in weakness."

O Beloved, do you see it? What God is saying to Paul He is saying to you. When you come under the discipline of the Lord, when God takes you through the refining process to make you into the image of His Son, know this: *His grace is sufficient.* It is enough! It is completely adequate! He will not give you more than you can bear. This is the promise of 1 Corinthians 10:13:

No temptation [trial or testing] has overtaken you but such as is common to man; and God is faithful, who will not allow you to be tempted beyond what you are able, but with the temptation will provide the way of escape also, that you may be able to endure it.

You can endure it because His grace is sufficient!
When then does bitterness come?
Bitterness comes
    when we fail to be meek,
    when we fail to submit to our Father's discipline,
    when we fail to give thanks in everything,
    when we come short of the grace of God.

If you are bitter, it is because someone has disappointed you or hurt you or misused you and you have been unable or unwilling to see that it had to come into your life through the filter of God's love. You have failed to see that God in His sovereignty permitted it. You have failed to bow the knee in meekness and say, "My Father, if it pleases You, it pleases me."

So how can you get rid of that root of bitterness?

It's as easy as confession and forgiveness.

But you say, "Kay, that's *not* easy." All right. Then it's as close as determined, willful obedience to God.

Will you obey?

Will you confess to God that you have fallen short of His grace? Will you confess that you have allowed a root of bitterness to spring up in you? And will you call upon God and ask Him to remove those pockets of poison in your soul and to fill you afresh with His Holy Spirit?

You must forgive.

To the very depths of your heart, you must fully forgive whoever has wounded you, deceived you, or transgressed against you.

"But I can't!" you say? No, Beloved, it's not that you can't but that you *won't*. There's a big difference. Know this: If you do not forgive others, God cannot forgive you. So you *can* forgive and you must forgive. The question is, will you?

Or if your complaint is against God, if you are bitter toward Him, then you need to ask Him to forgive you for your lack of meekness.

Meekness is the sure cure for bitterness…bitterness toward God or bitterness toward man. It is strong medicine indeed. And though it may be hard medicine to swallow in some cases, once you have ingested it, you will taste the sweet, healing flavor of life itself.

Now then, Beloved, ask God to show you any root of bitterness in your heart that needs uprooting. Tell Him you want it gone. Give Him permission to remove it—even if the roots are deep! Then wait on Him in prayer. In the space below, write out anything and everything He puts in your heart to do.

Have you done it? Then consider yourself *blessed*, meek one.

MEMORY VERSE

> Come to Me, all who are weary and heavy-laden, and I will give you rest. Take My yoke upon you, and learn from Me, for I am gentle and humble in heart; and YOU SHALL FIND REST FOR YOUR SOULS. For My yoke is easy, and My load is light.
>
> MATTHEW 11:28-30

SMALL-GROUP DISCUSSION QUESTIONS

1. What new insights have you gained concerning meekness?
2. How did Jesus display meekness? Is meekness really just weakness?
3. Have the class recite this week's memory verses: Matthew 11:28-30.
4. From where does meekness come? What is the source?
5. How is meekness toward God demonstrated in a person's behavior? How is meekness toward men demonstrated?
6. What is the relationship of meekness to humility?
7. Does the thought of accepting and submitting to God's authority in your life scare you? What causes this fear? How can you handle it?
8. How is meekness related to righteous indignation? Can the meek experience anger? Explain.

9. What is the relationship of meekness to weakness? If we are meek, are we doormats? Explain.
10. Explain the relationship of bitterness to meekness.
11. What effect does bitterness have? What must you do with bitterness? If you don't, what will bitterness do to you?
12. Do you see God changing you?

HUNGERING AND THIRSTING FOR RIGHTEOUSNESS

— D A Y O N E —

The words "Sermon on the Mount" sound traditional and respectable now.

You visualize the words written in flowing, Old English script. You see the scene in your mind's eye as through a stained glass window, with gentle, colored light flowing through two-dimensional images. It all seems very calm and serene and conventional.

Yet when Jesus delivered those words, they were like lightning bolts out of a blue sky. They shook the carefully constructed foundations of religion and knocked people off their feet. It was radical, revolutionary teaching. Power surged through those words, leaving the listeners shocked and stunned.

It was *anything but* calm, conventional, and traditional.

Why? Because the Teacher from Galilee called for a righteousness that exceeded the righteousness of the scribes and Pharisees (Matthew 5:20). He redefined true blessedness or happiness. It was not a happiness based on fickle circumstances but a happiness that bubbled up from deep inner wells *because of who they were!*

It was not for the proudly independent.

It was not for the confidently self-righteous.

It was not for the aggressive traditionalist.

No, this was a blessedness for the poor in spirit and for mourners. It was a deep satisfaction, a contentment of soul for the meek, the hungry, the merciful, the pure in heart, the peacemakers, and the persecuted.

The men and women who heard these words could hardly believe their ears! Could it be? If these things were true, it could turn their whole world upside down!

As a matter of fact, it did.

The Sermon on the Mount explains the *true* intent of the Law…a law that reaches beyond external obedience to the heart…a law that cancels the natural responses of men and calls for supernatural behavior. That's why Jesus said, "Be perfect, therefore, as your heavenly Father is perfect" (Matthew 5:48, NIV).

In Matthew 6, Jesus reevaluated true piety and godliness. He spoke of a righteousness that was genuine to the core. This was a righteousness that was not to be paraded before the eyes of others, but was for God's eyes and praise alone! Jesus caused His hearers to examine the thrust of their lives. What were true treasures? Who was their true master? For whom were they spending their lives and energies?

According to Matthew 7, Jesus knew that righteousness could lead to hypocritical judging. So He carefully warned His listeners to make sure that they took the beams out of their own eyes before they sought to take the specks out of their brothers' eyes. He wanted them to know that those who have inherited the kingdom of heaven need only ask, seek, and knock. After all, God was now their Father, and it was His delight to give them bounty from His hand. Finally in Matthew 7:12, Jesus gave them the true interpretation of the Law and the Prophets in a single sentence: "Therefore, however you want people to treat you, so treat them, for this is the Law and the Prophets."

Then came the invitation to enter in by the narrow gate. They need not be shocked by the news that few would find it, for most would go by the broad way that led to destruction. In a few brief words the Teacher set before His amazed listeners two ways, two gates, two responses, and two fruits. He showed them that the kingdom of heaven does not belong to those who call Him "Lord, Lord" but to those who live under His lordship. Hearing and obeying bring righteousness.

What would those listeners do with such radical words? As it turned out, they would either walk away, shaking their heads in disbelief, or they would find themselves possessed by an intense hunger and thirst for more. A hunger and thirst for righteousness.

This is our topic of study for the week. "Blessed are those who hunger and thirst for righteousness, for they shall be satisfied" (Matthew 5:6).

What I have just given you is a brief overview of the Sermon on the Mount. It's important that you keep it in mind so that you are able to see each beatitude in the context of the whole Sermon.

Your assignment today is to read through Matthew 5, 6, and 7. As you do, remember this overview and note how it capsulizes the content of the Sermon on the Mount. Then go to your Father and ask Him to show you what it really means to hunger and thirst after righteousness. Briefly write down what He shows you.

— D A Y   T W O —

What does it mean to hunger and thirst after righteousness?

Hunger and thirst are bodily cravings that must be satisfied if life is to be sustained. And there, Beloved, is the key. The Sermon on the Mount clearly shows us that unless we have a righteousness that surpasses the righteousness of the scribes and Pharisees, we shall in no way attain eternal life. The Sermon on the Mount is all about the righteous lifestyle of those who belong to the kingdom of heaven.

To what degree, then, are we to desire this righteousness? To the same degree that we hunger after food and thirst after water! If we are going to have a righteousness that will bring life, then we must crave it with the *intensity* of hunger and thirst.

Perhaps you are thinking, "That certainly eliminates a lot of people, doesn't it?"

Yes, it does.

Now you can understand why Jesus says that the way is very narrow and the gate is very small!

Hunger and *thirst* are present active participles which show us that hungering and thirsting for righteousness is not a one-time action, but a continual habit of life. Just as one meal does not satisfy you for the rest of your life or even for the rest of the week, so one initial hungering and thirsting for righteousness cannot satisfy you for life. It is to be a day-by-day occurrence. That is why Jesus chose the words *hunger* and *thirst*— they are cravings common to all mankind. Everyone understands them.

Now then, Beloved, is there a hunger and thirst for God within you, a deep craving for righteousness? If not, it could be that you've not yet been born of God's Spirit, so please listen carefully.

The word for *righteousness* in the Greek is used of whatever is right or just in itself and therefore conforms to the revealed will of God. Let me give you some expanded definitions which will help you gain a fuller understanding of what God means.

Righteousness is whatever God decrees man to acknowledge and obey. Note: It is what *God says,* not what *man thinks!* Righteousness is the sum total of the requirements of God.

Righteousness is also used to refer to an individual's religious duties. We see this in Matthew 6, where Jesus tells us to beware of practicing our righteous acts, such as giving, praying, and fasting, in order to be seen by others.

Finally, as we have seen before, righteousness is an attribute of God. It is the very essence of God's being. To hunger and thirst after righteousness is to have a deep, inner longing to please God. It is a longing that God Himself plants within our hearts to cause us to seek after Him. To hunger and thirst after righteousness is to desire with all our being to live and walk the way God says to live and walk.

It is to *crave* God.

It is to *crave* holiness.

Now, may I ask you again? Do you hunger and thirst after righteousness?

Your answer may be, "Kay, I'm not sure." Before this week is finished, Beloved, we'll be talking about how you can know for sure if it's there. If it is, you'll find out what you can do to increase it. And if it's not, I fervently pray that God will show you how it can be there.

In the United States of America it is hard for most of us to understand the intensity of these two words, *hungering* and *thirsting*. We live in a land of abundance. We have lots of drinking fountains, an ample supply of soft drink machines, restaurants, and fast-food places on every corner. Yet if we could go back to Jesus' day, we would meet a people who really understood what it was like to have an intense craving for food and an overwhelming thirst for water. Often, parched lips blessed God for wells that brought welcome relief from the intense heat of the Judean hills. And if they'd neglected to carry food with them, there was no place to pick some up along the way.

How I remember being moved as I read the biography of Pastor Hsi, a man who survived the horrible famine that devastated the provinces of North China in 1878. At that time he had not yet become a Christian. He had been a proud and highly respected Confucian scholar, sought out within his community for his wisdom. In the course of time, he contracted a horrible illness that left his body racked with pain. His friends urged him to try opium for relief.

Hsi, however, had witnessed the havoc wrought by the opium habit. He lived among men who had been literally destroyed by opium and were totally worthless to society. How could he turn in such a direction?

Yet his pain intensified until it seemed intolerable. Could anything be worse?

"You need not smoke it constantly," his friends told him. "Just take a little until you are better. Then it will be quite easy to give it up."

So Hsi yielded and in his yielding eventually became an opium addict. When the famine hit in 1878, he managed to survive because he grew opium, and men would sell their very souls to support their habits.

The famine was mind-boggling in its devastation. Over seventy million human beings were starving. "During that journey," one man recorded, "we saw scenes that have left an indelible impression of horror on the mind." He went on:

> We passed men, once strong and well-dressed, staggering over the frozen ground with only a few rags to shield them from the piercing wind. Their feeble steps, emaciated bodies and wild looks told only too plainly that they were about to spend their last night upon earth. As we passed along the road in the early morning we saw the victims of the preceding night lying dead and stiff where they fell. Upon that road we saw men writhing in the last agonies of death. No one pitied them; no one cared for them; such sights had long ago become too common. There were hundreds of corpses lying by the roadside.... Families were broken up; the wife sold; the children sold or cast out on the mountainside to perish, while the men wandered about in the vain search for food. The whole district through which we passed (three or four hundred miles) was in the same condition.[1]

It was so bad that men did not go out in the streets alone lest someone attack them, kill them, and drag them home to eat them.

Early in 1878 the *London Times* carried this report:

> It is stated on authority which cannot be questioned, that seventy millions of human beings are now starving in the famine-stricken provinces

of North China. The imagination fails to cope with a calamity so gigantic. The inhabitants of the United Kingdom and the United States combined hardly number seventy millions. To think of the teeming populations of these lands, all crowded into an area very little greater than that of France, starving and eating earth, with no food to be had, and with no hope of succour, is enough to freeze the mind with horror.[2]

This, Beloved, is the intense hunger that God is talking about. This is not a hunger that stands at the open door of a full refrigerator, trying to decide if anything looks appealing. This is not a hunger that debates whether it can handle a third helping. *This is a hunger that has to have food or it dies.*

Pastor Hsi is a living example of one who hungered and thirsted after righteousness. Under the direction of Hudson Taylor, the China Inland Mission sent missionaries into North China. In his desire to reach the Confucian scholars, one of these missionaries offered a cash prize to those who would propound six theses on various biblical subjects. Each contestant would be supplied a packet of Christian books and tracts so that he might thoroughly study the subject. The winner would have to appear in person in order to collect his prize of silver. Hsi won every prize! As a result, the missionary invited Hsi to become his translator. Hsi found himself thrust continually into the Word of God. That, plus the fact that he lived in the missionary's house, was God's means of drawing Hsi into His kingdom.

We'll read a little more about this remarkable Chinese pastor, but before we do, let's look again at the first four beatitudes.

"Blessed are the poor in spirit…"

"Blessed are those that mourn…"

"Blessed are the meek…"

"Blessed are those who hunger and thirst for righteousness…"

There is a definite order here, isn't there? We can see the progression of God's work in our hearts as we come to Him. As you read the next few paragraphs, note in the margin any manifestations of the Beatitudes you see in Pastor Hsi's life.

Gradually as he [Hsi] read, the life of Jesus seemed to grow more real and full of interest and wonder, and he began to understand that this mighty Savior was no mere man as he had once imagined, but God, the very God, taking upon Him mortal flesh. Doubts and difficulties were lost sight of. The old, unquenchable desire for better things, for deliverance from sin, self, and the fear of death, for light upon the dim, mysterious future, came back upon him as in earlier years. And yet the burden of his guilt, the torment of an accusing conscience, and bondage to the opium-habit he loathed but could not conquer, grew more and more intolerable.

At last the consciousness of his unworthiness became so overwhelming that he could bear it no longer and placing the Book [the Bible] reverently before him, he fell upon his knees on the ground, and with so many tears followed the sacred story. It was beginning then to dawn upon his soul that this wonderful, divine, yet human Sufferer, in all the anguish of His bitter cross and shame, had something personally to do with him, with his sin and sorrow and need.

And so, upon his knees, the once proud, self-satisfied Confucianist read on until he came to "the place called Gethsemane," and the God man, alone, in that hour of His supreme agony at midnight in the Garden. Then the fountains of his long-sealed heart were broken up. The very presence of God overshadowed him. In the silence he seemed to hear the Savior's cry—"My soul is exceedingly sorrowful, even unto death": and into his heart there came the wonderful realization—"He loved me, and gave Himself for me." Then, suddenly, as he himself records, the Holy Spirit influenced his soul, and "with tears that flowed and would not cease" he bowed and yielded himself, unreservedly, to the world's Redeemer, as his Savior and his God....

He saw Him then, not only as his Savior, but as his absolute Owner, his Master, his Lord....

Immediately upon his conversion the conviction came clearly to the scholar's mind that his opium-habit must at once be broken. There seems to have been no parleying about it. Ever since he first entered the missionary's household, his conscience had troubled him on the subject....

But at that time he knew of no power that could enable him to cleanse himself from the degrading vice. Now all was different. He belonged to Christ, and there could be no doubt as to the will of his new Master.... Of course he knew well what leaving off opium-smoking would involve. But there was no shrinking; no attempt at half measures. He saw it must be sacrificed at once, entirely, and forever. Then came the awful conflict....

As hour after hour went by, his craving for the poison became more intense than the urgency of hunger or thirst. Acute anguish seemed to render the body asunder, accompanied by faintness and exhaustion that nothing could relieve. Water streamed from the eyes and nostrils. Extreme depression overwhelmed him. Giddiness came on, with shivering, and aching pains, or burning thirst. For seven days and nights he scarcely tasted food and was quite unable to sleep. Sitting or lying he could get no rest. The agony became almost unbearable; and all the while he knew that a few whiffs of the opium-pipe would waft him at once into delicious dreams....

At last, in the height of his distress, it seemed to be revealed to him that the anguish that he was suffering arose not merely from physical causes, but that behind it all lay concealed the opposition of some mighty spiritual force; that he was in fact, hard pressed by the devil, who was using this opium craving as a weapon for his destruction....

Then how utterly did the helpless man cast himself on God. Refusing to be dragged away one step from his only refuge, he fought out the battle in the very presence of his new-found Savior....

"Devil, what can you do against me? My life is in the hands of God.

And truly I am willing to break off opium and die, but not willing to continue in sin and live!"

In his most suffering moments he would frequently groan out loud: "Though I die, I will never touch it again!"

At last, after many days of anguish, his attention was attracted by some verses in his open Bible telling about "the Comforter"; and, as he read, it was borne in upon his mind that He, the Holy Spirit of God, was the mighty power expressly given to strengthen men. Then and there, in utter weakness, he cast himself on God.... He did not understand much, but he had grasped the supreme fact that the Holy Spirit could help him, making impossible things possible, and overcoming all the power of the enemy. And there as he prayed in the stillness, the wonderful answer was given. Suddenly a tide of life and power seemed to sweep into his soul.... The Holy Spirit came, flooding his heart with peace.[3]

This, Beloved, is what it means to hunger and thirst after righteousness. It means that you just have to be right with God—no matter what it costs! It is a craving that must be satisfied if life is to be sustained! Think about it. What do you absolutely *have* to have? What do you hunger for? Thirst for?

— D A Y   T H R E E —

As we come to this fourth beatitude, "Blessed are those who hunger and thirst for righteousness," we reach a pinnacle in our relationship with God.

The first four beatitudes—poverty of spirit, mourning, meekness, and hungering and thirsting for righteousness—are certainly directed toward God. And it seems that this hungering and thirsting for righteousness then becomes the forward thrust for the beatitudes that follow: desiring to be merciful, pure in heart, a peacemaker, and as a result, being persecuted. I have included a little diagram to illustrate.

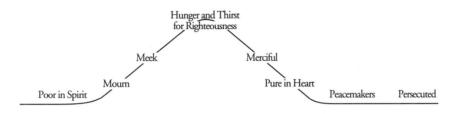

British expositor Martyn Lloyd-Jones said this of hungering and thirsting after righteousness:

> This beatitude follows logically from the previous ones; it is a statement to which all the others lead. It is the logical conclusion to which they come and it is something for which we should all be profoundly thankful and grateful to God. I do not know of a better test that anyone can apply to himself or herself in this whole matter of the Christian profession than a verse like this. If this verse is to you one of the most blessed statements of the whole of Scripture you can be quite sure you are a Christian; if it is not, then you had better examine the foundations again.[4]

There are two kinds of righteousness. It is important that we know which is which so that we don't become confused and think we have the genuine when we do not. To do so would be to miss the kingdom of heaven!

The distinction is really quite simple. There is a self-righteousness, and there is a righteousness that comes from God.

Self-righteousness means living by your version of what you think is required of man. In the Sermon on the Mount, Jesus deals pointedly with this kind of righteousness. He does it repeatedly in chapter 5 when He says "You have heard...but I say to you...." They *had* heard from the scribes and Pharisees about a certain code of righteousness to which they must adhere. Jesus pulled the rug out from under those false standards! And then He laid the shining truth at their very feet.

The righteousness of the scribes and Pharisees was a self-righteousness. God's righteousness went far beyond self-righteousness.

That's why in Matthew 23 Jesus constantly says, "Woe to you, scribes and Pharisees!" They were only keeping God's Law to the limit of their own desires. Theirs was an external, not an internal, righteousness. This couldn't be more clear than when Jesus said, "Woe to you, scribes and Pharisees, hypocrites! For you tithe mint and dill and cummin, and have neglected the weightier provisions of the law: justice and mercy and faithfulness; but these are the things you should have done without neglecting the others" (Matthew 23:23).

For the most part, the nation of Israel followed in the footsteps of the scribes and Pharisees. This is why Paul chose to write such strong words in Romans 10:1-3:

> Brethren, my heart's desire and my prayer to God for them is for their salvation. For I bear them witness that they have a zeal for God, but not in accordance with knowledge. For not knowing about God's righteousness, and seeking to establish their own, they did not subject themselves to the righteousness of God.

Do you see the contrast?

They were depending on their *own* righteousness instead of God's righteousness!

What about you? What kind of righteousness do you have? Is it your own...or is it God's? Do you live by your own set of dos and don'ts, your own little code of righteousness? Because you do certain things, or because you don't do certain things, do you consider yourself righteous? And do you judge the righteousness of others by your code?

In our area of the country, some people have evaluated women over the years according to the length of their skirts. Men were evaluated by the length of their hair. Issues such as movie-going or card-playing or frequency of church attendance found their way onto the "righteousness scorecard."

These dos and don'ts, of course, change with the passing of years. Which is precisely the point! They are external, changing standards which compose an artificial, man-centered standard of righteousness. But what's the real issue? It's what's happening in men's and women's hearts!

What's going on in the *hearts* of those who set up these various legalistic codes and lists of dos and don'ts? Do they judge and criticize others? Do they cut them down or murder them with their tongues? What kinds of thoughts are harbored in the mind, in the heart? If the heart does not match the outward performance, then it is a case of self-righteousness. It is a righteousness lived by the letter of the Law rather than a righteousness based on faith. And those sorts of hollow, external evaluations made God's Son very angry!

Self-righteousness is always man's interpretation or addition to the clear-cut teaching of God's Word. It's a process of tacking on extra laws, requirements, and expectations, and then saying that if you are *really* going to be righteous, you must keep all these rules. It is judging others by your standards rather than God's. How deceptive this is, Beloved! What a terrible trap it becomes!

Those who chase after these external requirements become blinded to the true, heart-transforming righteousness based on faith alone. Let me say it again: Self-righteousness is living by your version of what you think is required by God and then imposing that standard on others, judging their righteousness by whether or not they march to the same drumbeat as you.

And what about God's righteousness? What a different story!

God's righteousness begins with a dissatisfaction, a yearning. When sin's presence within is finally realized, an inner longing is kindled and begins to burn with a slow, steady flame. A longing to be righteous! With every glimpse of God's shining holiness and purity comes an accompanying awareness of self (just as the prophet experienced in Isaiah 6). *I'm unclean! I've fallen short of God's standard of perfection! I've left undone what ought to have been done, and I've done that which should never have been done! All of my righteousness is as filthy rags in God's sight.*

Finally the realization comes: "God, You alone are righteous." A hunger and thirst for righteousness—His righteousness—awakens and grows. But how is that hunger and thirst to be satisfied? We know we cannot quench it in ourselves, so we run to the fountain of living waters and receive the gift of the indwelling Holy Spirit. He alone can lead us into a life of righteousness, by leading us into the truth.

It was for just that reason that Jesus stood and cried out on the last day of the Feast of Tabernacles. During this great feast the people went to the pool of Siloam each day for seven days, filling pitchers with water. Then, as they walked to the temple, they sang Psalms 103 through 118. Arriving at the temple, they would pour the water on the altar, symbolizing both the early and latter rains and the outpouring of the Holy Spirit promised in the Old Testament.

> Now on the last day, the great day of the feast, Jesus stood and cried out, saying, "If any man is thirsty, let him come to Me and drink. He who believes in Me, as the Scripture said, 'From his innermost being shall flow rivers of living water.'" But this He spoke of the Spirit, whom those who believed in Him were to receive; for the Spirit was not yet given, because Jesus was not yet glorified. (John 7:37-39)

It's interesting to note that when Jesus said, "Let him come to Me and drink," the verbs *come* and *drink* are in the present tense. It literally means, "Let him *keep coming* to Me and let him *keep drinking*."

Jesus is the fountainhead of God's righteousness. O Beloved, do you see it? You can be as righteous as you want to be! How? By totally depending upon God. By yearning for Him more and more.

Ours is to be an ever-increasing hunger and thirst. The more we get, the more we want; the more we want, the more we get.

Pay careful attention now as we wrap up today's study. Jesus illustrates this ever-increasing hunger and thirst for righteousness in the parable of the sower in Matthew 13. "For whoever has," Jesus says, "to him shall more be given, and he shall have an abundance; but whoever does not have, even what he has shall be taken away from him" (verse 12).

What did He mean? He had just told the parable. He had just revealed that only one type of soil—*good* soil—yielded a crop.

What made the difference? It wasn't the seed, because Jesus tells us in Matthew 13:19 that the seed is the word of the kingdom, the truth of righteous living. It was *the soil's receptivity to the seed* that made the difference. Mark 4:20 adds clarity here: "And those are the ones on whom seed was sown on the good soil; and they hear the word and accept it, and bear fruit, thirty, sixty, and a hundredfold."

Did you notice the words "accept it"? Why don't you underline them. Obviously the more we accept, the greater the crop will be. That's why Jesus goes on to say in Mark 4:24-25: "Take care what you listen to. By your standard of measure it shall be measured to you; and more shall be given you besides. For whoever has, to him shall more be given; and whoever does not have, even what he has shall be taken away from him."

Do you want to be righteous? *Then receive what God has for you.* Be obedient to the revealed will of God, not just with an external obedience, but from the heart. God will give you more and more. But neglect His Word, ignore it, or refuse it, and you will have a meager harvest.

As we close today, I want you to read Psalm 63:1-5, printed below, and meditate on it in the light of this fourth beatitude and all that you have learned so far. Then pray those verses back to God, making them the very cry of your heart.

O God, Thou art my God; I shall seek Thee earnestly;
My soul thirsts for Thee, my flesh yearns for Thee,
In a dry and weary land where there is no water.
Thus I have beheld Thee in the sanctuary,
To see Thy power and Thy glory.
Because Thy lovingkindness is better than life,
My lips will praise Thee.

So I will bless Thee as long as I live;

I will lift up my hands in Thy name.

My soul is satisfied as with marrow and fatness,

And my mouth offers praises with joyful lips.

— D A Y   F O U R —

How can you be sure that you have a genuine hunger and thirst for God's righteousness?

First of all, you will be aware of a longing for God and His Word. Read the following passages and underline words or phrases which indicate a longing, a desire, or a determination to achieve or attain something.

◗ PSALM 42:1-2

1 As the deer pants for the water brooks,

So my soul pants for Thee, O God.

2 My soul thirsts for God, for the living God;

When shall I come and appear before God?

◗ PSALM 27:4

One thing I have asked from the LORD, that I shall seek:

That I may dwell in the house of the LORD all the days of my life,

To behold the beauty of the LORD,

And to meditate in His temple.

What was the psalmist desiring? To what degree?

According to Psalm 27:4, what was the "one thing" David desired above all else?

Was it a passive desire? How do you know?

The words *law, judgments, precepts, statutes, commandments,* and *testimonies* are all references to the Word of God. What do you note in the following verses about the psalmist and his relationship to God and His Word?

▶ PSALM 119:1-8,40,123

How blessed are those whose way is blameless,
Who walk in the law of the LORD.
How blessed are those who observe His testimonies,
Who seek Him with all their heart.
They also do no unrighteousness;
They walk in His ways.
Thou hast ordained Thy precepts,
That we should keep them diligently.
Oh that my ways may be established
To keep Thy statutes!
Then I shall not be ashamed
When I look upon all Thy commandments.
I shall give thanks to Thee with uprightness of heart,
When I learn Thy righteous judgments.
I shall keep Thy statutes;
Do not forsake me utterly!...

Behold, I long for Thy precepts;
Revive me through Thy righteousness....
My eyes fail with longing for Thy salvation,
And for Thy righteous word.

Second, when you have a genuine hunger and thirst for righteousness, you will hate sin. You cannot love both righteousness and sin; they are incompatible. Therefore, you will hate wickedness and sin because it keeps you from righteousness. Psalm 45:6-7 says:

Thy throne, O God, is forever and ever;
A scepter of uprightness is the scepter of Thy kingdom.
Thou hast loved righteousness, and hated wickedness.

Righteousness loves the things God loves and hates the things God hates.

Psalm 101 sets forth God's standards of righteousness in graphic detail. Read the psalm, printed out below.

 PSALM 101

I will sing of lovingkindness and justice,
To Thee, O LORD, I will sing praises.
I will give heed to the blameless way.
When wilt Thou come to me?
I will walk within my house in the integrity of my heart.
I will set no worthless thing before my eyes;

I hate the work of those who fall away;
It shall not fasten its grip on me.
A perverse heart shall depart from me;
I will know no evil.
Whoever secretly slanders his neighbor, him I will destroy;
No one who has a haughty look and an arrogant heart will I endure.
My eyes shall be upon the faithful of the land, that they may dwell
    with me;
He who walks in a blameless way is the one who will minister to me.
He who practices deceit shall not dwell within my house;
He who speaks falsehood shall not maintain his position before me.
Every morning I will destroy all the wicked of the land,
So as to cut off from the city of the LORD all those who do iniquity.

List the six things the psalmist has determined to do because he wants to walk blamelessly (righteously) before God. (Look for the six "I will" statements.)

1.

2.

3.

4.

5.

6.

The *third* and last evidence of the presence of righteousness is a longing to do God's will. If you are genuinely hungering and thirsting after righteousness, you must know and walk in obedience to the will of God.

The highest example of hungering and thirsting for righteousness is seen in Jesus when He says, "My food is to do the will of Him who sent Me, and to accomplish His work" (John 4:34).

What about you, my friend? What is your food? Calling Jesus "Lord" is not a guarantee of true righteousness, but honoring Him as Lord, longing to do His will, is. This is why Jesus says, "Not everyone who says to Me, 'Lord, Lord,' will enter the kingdom of heaven; but he who does the will of My Father who is in heaven" (Matthew 7:21).

If the Holy Spirit is truly within, you will hunger and thirst for righteousness. You will know He is there because you will have a longing for God and His Word. You will love righteousness and hate sin. You will long to do His will.

Now…where do you stand? Is the kingdom of heaven yours? It all begins with poverty of spirit. It begins with realizing how far short you fall of His righteous standards—and how all your self-righteousness is nothing more than filthy rags. You need to fall prostrate at the feet of God and say:

> *God, I have no righteousness of my own. There is no way that I could ever please You in and of myself. God, I have walked in independence and have lived my own life. I abhor myself and my actions and I turn to You. I am a sinner. Save me; set me apart for Yourself. Fill me with Your righteousness.*

O Beloved, if that is your heart's cry, God will not turn you away. Walk into His open arms and record this as the day of your salvation. Write out your prayer of commitment below.

— D A Y   F I V E —

The last thing we want to look at this week, Beloved, is a list of seven things you can do to increase your hunger and thirst for righteousness. As we begin, will you pray with the psalmist?

Search me, O God, and know my heart;
Try me and know my anxious thoughts;
And see if there be any hurtful way in me,
And lead me in the everlasting way.
(Psalm 139:23-24)

#1: BEWARE OF IDOLS

If you are going to have an increasing hunger and thirst for righteousness, you must first get rid of the idols in your heart. An idol is anything that stands between you and God and keeps you from following Him fully. It is anything that usurps the rightful place of God so that God no longer has preeminence in your life. Idols do not necessarily have six heads and twenty-four arms! They can be much more subtle and sophisticated than some crude stone statue with a ruby in its navel. Idols can also be television sets, houses, golf clubs, or careers. Idolatry can come in the form of a man, a woman, a child, a hope, a dream, or an ambition.

Note what Ezekiel 14:3 says, "Son of man, these men have set up their idols in *their hearts,* and have put right before their faces the stumbling block of their iniquity" (italics mine). When you love and serve something or someone more than you love and serve God, it is an idol. There is One and only One who is to govern our passions, our desires, and our energy, and that is our Lord and King.

If then you have been raised up with Christ, keep seeking the things above, where Christ is, seated at the right hand of God. Set your mind on the things above, not on the things that are on earth. (Colossians 3:1-2)

Are there any idols in your heart that are keeping you from hungering and thirsting after righteousness? If so, list them below and then, in prayer, smash them at the feet of God.

#2: TURN YOUR EYES FROM THE WORLD

I love pretty things, and if I didn't watch myself, I could get so caught up in them! Can you relate, my friend? The things of this world can be so appealing to our eyes, so attractive to our flesh. Therefore, if you and I want to increase our hunger and thirst for righteousness, we must be very careful what we allow before our eyes. God's warning is clear. He knows us!

> Do not love the world, nor the things in the world. If anyone loves the world, the love of the Father is not in him. For all that is in the world, the lust of the flesh and the lust of the eyes and the boastful pride of life, is not from the Father, but is from the world. (1 John 2:15-16)

In Matthew 6:22, Jesus tells us that the lamp of the body is the eye. We need to sing the same chorus that the little children sing in Sunday school, don't we?

> Be careful little eyes what you see;
> Be careful little eyes what you see;

For the Father up above is looking down in love,
So be careful little eyes what you see.

The psalmist's prayer captures this desire for purity of vision. Will you pray this prayer with him now?

Turn away my eyes from looking at vanity,
And revive me in Thy ways.
Establish Thy word to Thy servant,
As that which produces reverence for Thee.
(Psalm 119:37-38)

#3: COUNT ALL BUT JESUS AS LOSS

Count all things as loss in comparison with the saving, transforming knowledge of Jesus Christ. Take a minute and read Philippians 3:7-10. As you do, you will see that hungering and thirsting after righteousness is not just a matter of forsaking certain things. It is a matter of embracing others —and One above all. As you read this portion, mark every occurrence of the pronoun "I." Now, if this passage expresses the desire of your heart, turn it into your own personal prayer to the Lord.

▶ PHILIPPIANS 3:7-10

7 But whatever things were gain to me, those things I have counted as loss for the sake of Christ.

8 More than that, I count all things to be loss in view of the surpassing value of knowing Christ Jesus my Lord, for whom I have suffered the loss of all things, and count them but rubbish in order that I may gain Christ,

9 and may be found in Him, not having a righteousness of my own

derived from the Law, but that which is through faith in Christ, the right-

eousness which comes from God on the basis of faith,

10 that I may know Him, and the power of His resurrection and the fel-

lowship of His sufferings, being conformed to His death.

#4: PURSUE ONE GOAL

This leads us to the fourth thing. You must be a pursuer of one thing. Take time (and I do mean take careful, thoughtful time) to read Luke 10:38-42, printed below, and answer the questions which follow.

 LUKE 10:38-42

Now as they were traveling along, He entered a certain village; and a woman named Martha welcomed Him into her home. And she had a sister called Mary, who moreover was listening to the Lord's word, seated at His feet. But Martha was distracted with all her preparations, and she came up to Him, and said, "Lord, do You not care that my sister has left me to do all the serving alone? Then tell her to help me." But the Lord answered and said to her, "Martha, Martha, you are worried and both-ered about so many things; but only a few things are necessary, really only one, for Mary has chosen the good part, which shall not be taken away from her."

1. What was Martha's problem?

2. What was Mary doing?

Did you notice that the very thing Martha was doing *for* Jesus drew her away from the Lord? That's what *distracted* means. And this can happen to you. You can become so busy, so involved in the work of the Lord, that you actually diminish your hunger and thirst for righteousness. Remember, *doing* is secondary in the Christian life. The primary thing is *being*. What you do will be worth only as much as who you are!

What was Jesus' word to Martha?

"Martha, Martha…you are worried and upset about many things, but only one thing is needed." (Luke 10:41, NIV)

There we have it! Only one thing is needed! As you see, it's a matter of choice.

"Mary has chosen what is better, and it will not be taken away from her." (Luke 10:42, NIV)

If you want to increase your hunger and thirst for righteousness, you need to pursue one thing: to "know Him, and the power of His resurrection and the fellowship of His sufferings, [and to become] conformed to His death" (Philippians 3:10).

I rise before dawn and cry for help;
I wait for Thy words.
My eyes anticipate the night watches,
That I may meditate on Thy word.
(Psalm 119:147-148)

#5: WATCH THE COMPANY YOU KEEP!

First Corinthians 15:33 gives this clear word: "Do not be deceived: 'Bad company corrupts good morals.'"

Righteousness is living morally according to God's standard. What friends do you have who distract you or pull you away from your pursuit of holiness? Remember the yoke we talked about when we studied meekness? Are you in a yoke with someone who is drawing you away from the Lord—keeping you away from His yoke? Listen to 2 Corinthians 6:17-18 to see what you ought to do.

> "Therefore, COME OUT FROM THEIR MIDST AND BE SEPARATE," says the Lord.… "And I will welcome you. And I will be a father to you."

#6: KEEP COMING TO HIM

Jesus is the fountainhead of all righteousness. Therefore, Beloved, we must keep coming to Him, the wellspring of righteous living. We saw this in John 7:37. I want you to see it again in Isaiah 55:1-3:

> Ho! Every one who thirsts, come to the waters;
> And you who have no money come, buy and eat.
> Come, buy wine and milk
> Without money and without cost.
> Why do you spend money for what is not bread,
> And your wages for what does not satisfy?
> Listen carefully to Me, and eat what is good,
> And delight yourself in abundance.
> Incline your ear and come to Me.
> Listen, that you may live.

Don't you love that line, "Why do you spend money for what is not bread, and your wages for what does not satisfy?" Doesn't that describe America? Have you ever just stood in the malls and watched the people hurrying…looking…desiring…whipping out that plastic and buying? Sometimes I stand there and I think, *Lord, how many of these people really know You?*

Oh, if only we would lay aside our stereo headphones and turn off the noise of the television and the radio…if we would leave the malls, get out of the stadiums, and go be alone and quiet before the Lord. If we would just come to Him, then we would find that satisfaction we so long for. He says to us:

I, the LORD, am your God,
Who brought you up from the land of Egypt;
Open your mouth wide and I will fill it.
(Psalm 81:10)

#7: RECEIVE WHAT HE GIVES YOU

Finally, Beloved, if you want to increase your hunger and thirst for righteousness, open your hands! Open your heart! Receive all that He has for you. Remember what He says in Matthew 13:12: "For whoever has, to him shall more be given.…"

Are you hungering and thirsting for righteousness? Is the hunger sharp and the thirst deep? Do you have a longing in your heart that grows with the passing weeks, months, and years?

If you do, I leave you with a promise uttered from the very throne of God.

"You will be satisfied."

MEMORY VERSE

Blessed are those who hunger and thirst for righteousness, for they shall be satisfied.

MATTHEW 5:6

SMALL-GROUP DISCUSSION QUESTIONS

1. Quote the beatitude for the week.
2. What does it mean to hunger and thirst after righteousness?
3. How would you define and illustrate righteousness?
4. What admonition did Jesus give to guard us against judging others hypocritically?
5. What analogies did Jesus use to illustrate the two responses to His invitation to enter the kingdom of heaven?
6. How is God's righteousness demonstrated in your life?
7. Do you have any areas of self-righteousness you need to let go? What happens to your heart when you judge others by self-righteous standards?
8. What seven things can you do to increase your hunger and thirst for righteousness?
9. Which of these seven is the most difficult for you to do? Why?

HOW CAN I BE MERCIFUL...PURE?

— D A Y   O N E —

He clutched his blanket tighter about him. His arms hugged his drawn-up knees, not so much to stop the trembling, but rather to put flesh next to flesh. Curled up like a ball, he sat in the corner of his damp, frigid cell.

He'd been so preoccupied with the cold he hadn't heard the approaching footsteps. Startled, he watched the form of a bleeding, beaten human being tossed in the opposite corner like a filthy rag.

His new cellmate was naked from the waist up. Sobbing, he slumped in his corner, head down. As the man surveyed the condition of his new cellmate, he thought, "He'll never make it through the night. He'll be dead by morning."

Then came that still, small, familiar voice. *Give him your blanket.*

"But, Lord...if I give him my blanket, I'll not survive the night!"

I know. But you will be with Me. Give him your blanket.

The human ball slowly stretched out, assuming the stature of a man. The blanket slipped from his bent shoulders. He walked stiffly across the cell and handed the man his blanket.

"Here. The Lord Jesus Christ told me to give you my blanket."

For the first time he saw the man's face. It was incredulous with hope.

That night, the giver of the blanket died. Another grain of wheat had fallen into the ground! The recipient, however, lived. And in later years, he told the story over and over again. He had found life through the loving mercy of another. He had not only found physical life but eternal life through the One who said, "Blessed are the merciful, for they shall receive mercy" (Matthew 5:7).

As we come to this fifth beatitude, you will notice that the remaining beatitudes take on a horizontal, people-to-people aspect. How do those who are poor in spirit respond to others? The answer is, with mercy because God has been merciful to them.

As Jesus set forth this beatitude before His disciples, He was not teaching them a new concept or a new condition for receiving mercy. The prophet had said long before, "With the merciful thou wilt shew thyself merciful" (2 Samuel 22:26, KJV).

Several different Hebrew words in the Old Testament are translated *mercy* and *merciful*. One of them depicts a heartfelt response by someone who gives to one in need. How well this is illustrated in the true story which I just told you. Another word sometimes translated *mercy* in the King James Version is rendered *kindness, lovingkindness, love, unfailing love,* or *loyalty* in other versions. Although there has been debate among scholars about how the word is to be translated, it is apparent that love, mercy, and kindness are intertwined and cannot be separated from one another.

The New Testament word for *merciful* means "not simply possessed of pity but actively compassionate."[1] Mercy then is "an outward manifestation of pity; it assumes need on the part of him who receives it, and the resources adequate to meet the need on the part of him who shows it."[2]

To a degree, we can show mercy in the strength of our own flesh. And yet that mercy will always be limited by our humanity. When we come to know Jesus Christ, we experience an endless reservoir of mercy, vast beyond comprehension. We are no longer constrained by our own meager resources.

True mercy has its origin in God. When we studied the character of God, we saw that one of His attributes was His mercy. In the light of this, I want to take time to share something very important—yet perhaps a little heavy and difficult to understand. Will you stay with me, Beloved? If you do, it will deepen your understanding and appreciation for mercy in a powerful way. You will see clearly how true mercy behaves.

Do you remember the tabernacle, or "tent of meeting," that Moses built under God's direction? Behind the veil, in the Holy of Holies, was the Ark of the Covenant, a box made of acacia wood and covered with gold. (See the drawing of the tabernacle below.)

On the top of that box was a lid called "the Mercy Seat." Inside the

THE TABERNACLE AND THE TRIBES OF ISRAEL

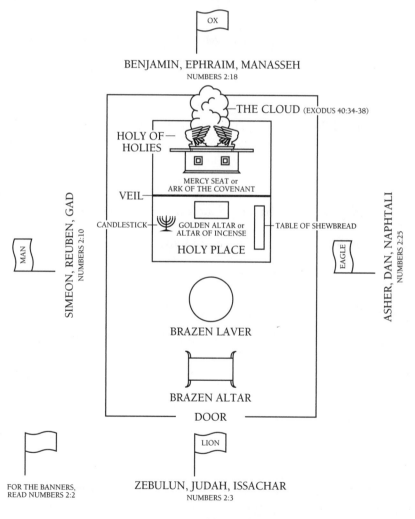

OX

BENJAMIN, EPHRAIM, MANASSEH
NUMBERS 2:18

—THE CLOUD (EXODUS 40:34-38)

HOLY OF—
HOLIES

MERCY SEAT or
ARK OF THE COVENANT

VEIL—

CANDLESTICK— GOLDEN ALTAR or
ALTAR OF INCENSE —TABLE OF SHEWBREAD

HOLY PLACE

SIMEON, REUBEN, GAD
NUMBERS 2:10

ASHER, DAN, NAPHTALI
NUMBERS 2:25

MAN

EAGLE

BRAZEN LAVER

BRAZEN ALTAR

DOOR

FOR THE BANNERS,
READ NUMBERS 2:2

ZEBULUN, JUDAH, ISSACHAR
NUMBERS 2:3

LION

EAST

Ark were the tables of stone which bore the Ten Commandments, Aaron's rod which had budded, and a pot of manna. When God looked down and saw those Ten Commandments which man had broken, it called forth His just judgment. Man was condemned because he had transgressed the Law. However, God, because of His love, made provision for a Mercy Seat, which covered the Ark of the Covenant.

Annually, on the Day of Atonement, the high priest would enter the Holy of Holies, once for his own sins and once again for the sins of the people. He would sprinkle the blood of a bull and a goat on the Mercy Seat to make an atonement (or a covering) for their sins. All of this was a picture, pointing to something that was to come. It was a foreshadowing of Jesus' sacrifice at Calvary.

Now let's look at some enlightening passages in the book of Hebrews. As you read this first passage, mark or underline the word *sacrifices*.

▶ HEBREWS 10:1-4

1 For the Law, since it has only a shadow of the good things to come and not the very form of things, can never by the same sacrifices year by year, which they offer continually, make perfect those who draw near.

2 Otherwise, would they not have ceased to be offered, because the worshipers, having once been cleansed, would no longer have had consciousness of sins?

3 But in those sacrifices there is a reminder of sins year by year.

4 For it is impossible for the blood of bulls and goats to take away sins.

This refers to the sacrifice I just explained to you. The Law, which required the sacrifice of the blood of bulls and goats, was a "shadow" or a picture of Jesus' blood, which would take away our sin (Hebrews 10:12).

Now look at another passage from Hebrews. As you read this passage, mark every reference to the high priest along with the synonyms or pronouns which refer to him. Take time to think through what the writer is saying about the person and duties of this high priest.

● HEBREWS 8:1-5

1 Now the main point in what has been said is this: we have such a high priest, who has taken His seat at the right hand of the throne of the Majesty in the heavens,

2 a minister in the sanctuary, and in the true tabernacle, which the Lord pitched, not man.

3 For every high priest is appointed to offer both gifts and sacrifices; hence it is necessary that this high priest also have something to offer.

4 Now if He were on earth, He would not be a priest at all, since there are those who offer the gifts according to the Law;

5 who serve a copy and shadow of the heavenly things, just as Moses was warned by God when he was about to erect the tabernacle; for, "SEE," He says, "THAT YOU MAKE all things ACCORDING TO THE PATTERN WHICH WAS SHOWN YOU ON THE MOUNTAIN."

From the above passage, how many tabernacles are there—and where is each?

We need to see that mercy has its origin in God. The earthly tabernacle that Moses pitched was patterned after the real or the true tabernacle in heaven. The Ark of the Covenant with the Mercy Seat was a picture of the throne of God. Do you see, Beloved? *God is showing us that the very essence of His being is mercy.*

A God of love and mercy sits upon that throne! Because man has transgressed God's holy Law, he stands condemned before God. And yet "God so loved the world, that He gave His only begotten Son, that whoever believes in Him should not perish, but have eternal life" (John 3:16). Because God is a God of love and a God of mercy, He took pity on man. He saw man's need and sent His Son to shed His blood on Calvary so that God's holiness might be "propitiated" or satisfied.

Have you ever heard of the doctrine of propitiation? In simple language, it means that Jesus' blood, shed at Calvary and applied to God's Mercy Seat, propitiates or satisfies the righteous, just, holy demands of God. Therefore in Luke 18:13 when the man cries out, "God be merciful to me a sinner" (KJV), it literally means "God be propitious to me a sinner."

Mercy is bonded with love—love's compassion which acts on behalf of the needy. So in love and mercy God sent His Son, Jesus, to die upon the cross. After His death, Jesus took His blood and, as the priest did on the Day of Atonement, appeared in the presence of the Father to put His blood on the Mercy Seat. God looked at that blood, and all the heavenly hosts sang, "Propitiated! Propitiated! God is satisfied!"

The Mercy Seat is the very throne of God, and mercy triumphs over judgment! Remember that, Beloved, because God is calling *you* to be merciful! He is calling you to be merciful, not only to the kind and attractive, not only to your friends and the people that you like, but even to those who sin against you.

We'll see it again in tomorrow's study. Today I just want you to see that it was out of mercy that God saved you. As you go to God in prayer, ask Him to open the eyes of your understanding so that you will walk in mercy, and so receive mercy.

– D A Y   T W O –

Jesus' life was a continuous manifestation of the mercy of God.

The Pharisees wanted to stone the woman who was caught in adultery, but Jesus, in mercy, pardoned her. When He saw the multitudes, "He felt compassion for them because they were like sheep without a shepherd" (Mark 6:34). Compassion moved Him to heal them, feed them, and teach them, for He knew that man does not live by bread alone but by every word that proceeds out of the mouth of God.

His mercy caused Him to call His disciples to plead with the Lord of the harvest to send out workers into His harvest. His life was a constant manifestation of the Godhead. If you had seen Him, you had seen the Father. And God always acts in mercy because He is merciful. For this reason, even when Jesus hung on the cross, listening to the taunts of those who had sought His death, in mercy He cried out, "Father, forgive them" (Luke 23:34).

Mercy meets the need of forgiveness.

How vital it is that you see this! Why? *Because unless you are merciful, you will not receive mercy.* And if you are going to be merciful, you must forgive others. Mercy and forgiveness are like Siamese twins with one heart. They can't be separated!

Matthew 18:21-35 makes this very clear. Take a few minutes to read these verses, printed out below. As you do, mark every use of the words *mercy, compassion, forgive,* and *forgave.* Also mark in distinguishing colors or ways the references to the two slaves, along with their respective pronouns. Then answer the questions which follow.

▶ MATTHEW 18:21-35

21 Then Peter came and said to Him, "Lord, how often shall my brother sin against me and I forgive him? Up to seven times?"

22 Jesus said to him, "I do not say to you, up to seven times, but up to seventy times seven.

23 For this reason the kingdom of heaven may be compared to a certain king who wished to settle accounts with his slaves.

24 And when he had begun to settle them, there was brought to him one who owed him ten thousand talents.

25 But since he did not have the means to repay, his lord commanded him to be sold, along with his wife and children and all that he had, and repayment to be made.

26 The slave therefore falling down, prostrated himself before him, saying, 'Have patience with me, and I will repay you everything.'

27 And the lord of that slave felt compassion and released him and forgave him the debt.

28 But that slave went out and found one of his fellow slaves who owed him a hundred denarii, and he seized him and began to choke him, saying, 'Pay back what you owe.'

29 So his fellow slave fell down and began to entreat him, saying, 'Have patience with me and I will repay you.'

30 He was unwilling however, but went and threw him in prison until he should pay back what was owed.

31 So when his fellow slaves saw what had happened, they were deeply grieved and came and reported to their lord all that had happened.

32 Then summoning him, his lord said to him, 'You wicked slave, I forgave you all that debt because you entreated me.

33 Should you not also have had mercy on your fellow slave, even as I had mercy on you?'

34 And his lord, moved with anger, handed him over to the torturers until he should repay all that was owed him.

35 So shall My heavenly Father also do to you, if each of you does not forgive his brother from your heart."

1. What particular situation prompted Jesus to tell this story?

2. List below all you observe about the two slaves from marking the text.

FIRST SLAVE   FELLOW SLAVE

3. Now read through this passage again and mark every reference to *king* or *lord*. What contrast do you see between the king's response to the slave who owed him money and the pardoned slave's response to his fellow slave who owed him money?

4. The following questions may seem redundant, but they really aren't. They will solidify the point of the whole story. Why was the king upset with the man he had forgiven? What did he do as a result?

5. Now, why did Jesus tell this story? What does He want us to learn? What does verse 35 teach us about God?

6. Finally, list below what you learn about mercy and being merciful.

This is a difficult passage, isn't it? It is especially difficult if there is someone we are not willing to really and truly forgive! It's hard because God is telling us that if we are not willing to forgive others, then God is not going to forgive us. We see the same thing in Matthew 6:15 which says, "But if you do not forgive men, then your Father will not forgive your transgressions."

I have seen people argue this point, saying it can't be, because that would make God's mercy conditional! But look again. What does the passage say? Put it alongside Matthew 5:7: "Blessed are the merciful, for they shall receive mercy." What does that imply? It implies that if you are not merciful toward others, you are not going to receive mercy yourself.

That *has* to be true. Otherwise, it means nothing to be blessed! If I can get mercy without being merciful, then why bother to be merciful? Mercy is not for the worthy; it's for the needy. And forgiveness is not based on worthiness.

Perhaps you're saying, "But you don't know how badly they have hurt me, Kay. You just have no idea because you don't know my story. You can't even imagine how unjustly I have been treated!"

Yes, Beloved, I can imagine. And I know how difficult this is. But let me take you back to God's throne. What is on it? A Mercy Seat. And that is where your sins were forgiven. When Jesus told the story in Matthew 18, He wanted to make a vivid point. The slave owed the king ten million dollars, and the king forgave it all. Are you sure you can't forgive? Are you sure you've experienced too much pain to be forgiving? What is your pain alongside His? Have you never seen what *your sin* did to the heart of perfect Holiness? And yet what came from His Throne? Love and mercy! As you have obtained mercy, will you not be merciful?

Please...don't read any further in this study until you have settled this issue with God.

Now let me share with you four practical ways that you can show mercy. To neglect any one of them is to fail to be merciful.

1. When you see a person in need and you can meet his needs, do so. (See James 2:15-16.)
2. Fully forgive anyone who is indebted to you in his behavior or attitude (see Colossians 3:12-15).
3. If you are going to be merciful, then you need to give understanding rather than judgment. Ask yourself, "Have I sat where they are living?" (See Ezekiel 3:15 and Luke 6:36-38.)
4. Be merciful toward the character of others. We all have different personalities, different temperament types. Therefore, you need to be merciful and respond to others in the light of their personality needs.

Some people need assurance. Give them assurance.
Some people are insecure. Affirm them.
Some people are weak. Support them.
Some people are timid. Encourage them.
Some people are reserved. Spur them on to love and good works. (See 1 Thessalonians 5:14-15; Hebrews 10:24.)

Have you ever read this greeting in Scripture: "Grace, mercy, and peace be unto you"? Grace is that unearned favor which saves us. Mercy is that undeserved favor which forgives us. And peace is that unsought favor which reconciles us. What a gracious and merciful God we have!

O Beloved, there is a whole world of broken, desperately wounded men, women, and children out there. Yes, many of them may be rude, crude, obnoxious, and self-centered. They're lost! They're despairing!

These are people who in no way deserve mercy…but need mercy desperately.

They are people who may not even understand they are unforgiven…but must find forgiveness or they will perish in their sins.

They need God's mercy and forgiveness. And Beloved, they need *your* mercy and forgiveness. Won't you tell God that you want to be merciful— even as He is merciful? Mercy, remember, is not for the worthy but the needy.

— *D A Y   T H R E E* —

Do you want to see God, see Him as He really is? Do you want to know Him intimately? Do you want to behold Him face to face someday? Then you must be pure in heart.

"Blessed are the pure in heart, *for they shall see God*" (Matthew 5:8, italics mine).

Purity of heart must precede the seeing. The mood of the Greek verb (indicative) for *see* means a certainty or a reality. You are going to be seeing God, and God is going to be seeing you! God promises it's going to happen.

If only the pure in heart are going to see God, then we need to know what it means to be pure. And we need to know what God means when He talks about the heart.

The word *pure* does not mean naturally pure; it means "pure as being cleansed." In other words, God is not saying that if I want to see Him, I have to have a heart that has never been dirty or tainted. Rather, it is a purity that comes from having been cleansed. Aren't you thankful? I am! Otherwise, I would *never* see God! I've been too dirty!

"The heart" can refer to several things. In this instance it refers to the seat of grief or joy, desires or affections, perceptions or thoughts, understanding or reasoning, imagination or conscience, intentions or purpose, will or faith.3 It is used in all these various ways in the New Testament. Therefore, when we speak of purity of heart, it is purity of actions, purity of thoughts, purity of desires and motivations, purity of proper reasoning. If I am going to have a pure heart, I am going to have to think properly and reason properly. This goes along with the Scripture: "as [a man] thinketh in his heart, so is he" (Proverbs 23:7, KJV). That is why you have to "watch over your heart with all diligence, for from it flow the springs of life" (Proverbs 4:23).

If you and I are going to see God continuously, then we must keep our hearts cleansed!

The question is…how?

First, let's look at the initial cleansing of our hearts that comes at salvation. According to the New Covenant of grace, God's Law is written in our hearts and we receive a new heart. Read the scriptures below, and mark every occurrence of the word *heart* with a ♡.

● JEREMIAH 31:33

"But this is the covenant which I will make with the house of Israel after those days," declares the LORD, "I will put My law within them, and on their heart I will write it; and I will be their God, and they shall be My people."

● EZEKIEL 36:26-27

26 "Moreover, I will give you a new heart and put a new spirit within you; and I will remove the heart of stone from your flesh and give you a heart of flesh.

27 "And I will put My Spirit within you and cause you to walk in My statutes, and you will be careful to observe My ordinances."

◗ 2 CORINTHIANS 3:2-3

2 You are our letter, written in our hearts, known and read by all men;

3 being manifested that you are a letter of Christ, cared for by us, written not with ink, but with the Spirit of the living God, not on tablets of stone, but on tablets of human hearts.

Second Corinthians 5:17 says, "If any man is in Christ, he is a new creature; the old things passed away; behold, new things have come."

If you know Jesus Christ as Lord and Savior, you *do* have a new heart. You *are* a new creation. Yet how do you live? Do you live in the light of the truth that your sins have been forgiven and God remembers them no more? Do you remember that your old self is dead and because of that, you have been freed from sin's power (Romans 6:6-7)? Discovering who you are in Christ Jesus and all that He has accomplished for you can radically transform your walk.

Now read the following verses and again mark every reference to the heart. Just draw a ♡.

◗ HEBREWS 10:19-22

19 Since therefore, brethren, we have confidence to enter the holy place by the blood of Jesus,

20 by a new and living way which He inaugurated for us through the veil, that is, His flesh,

21 and since we have a great priest over the house of God,

22 let us draw near with a sincere heart in full assurance of faith, having our hearts sprinkled clean from an evil conscience and our bodies washed with pure water.

These verses talk about us walking through the veil into the Holy Place, or the Holy of Holies. In this passage we see that we enter the Holy of Holies by the blood of Jesus. If the high priest tried to enter without a blood sacrifice, God would kill him. We saw in Hebrews 8 that the tabernacle on earth is a picture, a type, or a shadow of the true tabernacle in heaven. To carry that picture further, the veil of the Hebrew tabernacle is a picture to us of the flesh of Jesus Christ (Hebrews 10:20). It stood between man and God.

This is the essential truth of John 14:6, when Jesus said, "I am the way, and the truth, and the life; no one comes to the Father, but *through* Me" (italics mine). That concept is also reflected in 1 Timothy 2:5, where Paul tells us that "there is one God, and one mediator also between God and men, the man Christ Jesus."

The only way you and I can come into the presence of God is through Jesus. No man can come to the Father but by Him. Jesus is the way to God and is, therefore, our High Priest.

The author of Hebrews is telling us that we can have confidence or boldness to enter into the presence of God and stand before the throne of mercy. Why? Because the blood of Jesus Christ has been put on that Mercy Seat! Therefore, since we have that confidence, we can draw near to God with a sincere heart in full assurance of faith.

You might say, "Oh no, Kay, I couldn't do that. I'm too filthy. My thoughts—my heart—would be repugnant to God."

And I would have to reply to you, "Beloved, if you're a Christian, that's not true. According to Hebrews 10:22 your heart has been sprinkled clean from an evil conscience, and your body has been washed with pure water. You've been purified, sanctified."

Look at Hebrews 10:14: "For by one offering He [Jesus] has perfected for all time those who are sanctified." Where does a pure heart begin so that you can continuously see and behold God? It begins with salvation. It begins with the sacrifice of the blood of the Lamb, the Lamb without spot or blemish (1 Peter 1:19).

Isn't that beautiful?

Isn't it exciting to know that God has cleansed your heart so that you might see Him! To put it another way, in salvation He removes your heart of stone and gives you a heart of flesh.

Why don't you spend time today worshiping God, thanking Him for His Mercy Seat and for the rent veil of His flesh which allows you to come to Him with a heart sprinkled clean from an evil conscience.

Do you know what I do sometimes, Beloved? I worship God by mentally walking through the tabernacle. Let me show you how.

First, I start at the altar of bronze which is a picture of the Cross of Jesus Christ. There I thank God for the Cross and all it means to me—the love of God who gave His only begotten Son, the willingness of Jesus to die for me. Then I move behind the altar to the laver and thank God for the daily cleansing I have through His pure Word. I thank Him that He has kept His Word pure and that it is a mirror, showing me my spots and blemishes so that I might be made clean through the washing of the water of the Word.

Then I enter into the holy place and stop at the table of shewbread on the right-hand side. I praise God for Jesus, who is the Bread of Life, telling God that I want to feast on Him daily. I thank Him for His body which was broken for me. Then I cross to the left side to the *menorah*, the seven-branched candlestick, thanking Jesus that He is the Light of the world and that I don't have to walk in darkness if I walk as He walked. I thank Him for taking me out of darkness and into His marvelous light. I tell Him that I want to be filled with the oil of His Spirit so that I might burn brightly for Him. Then I walk to the altar of incense. I thank God that I have a great High Priest who ever lives to make intercession for me. I praise Him that He is a high priest who really feels my own weaknesses and infirmities, who was in every way tempted as I am, yet without sin. And I thank Him that because of His intercession He is able to save forever those who draw near to Him.

Then, looking at the veil, I think of His flesh torn in two, the sacrifice of the New Covenant. Prostrate, I thank Him for the new and living way He has opened, allowing me to enter into the very presence of the Almighty God, whom I can now call "Abba, Father." Standing before the Ark of the Covenant, I praise God for His throne and for the character of the One who sits upon the throne. I join the cherubim and the seraphim and the twenty-four elders as they "do not cease to say, 'HOLY, HOLY, HOLY, is THE LORD GOD, THE ALMIGHTY, who was and who is and who is to come.'... 'Worthy art Thou, our Lord and our God, to receive glory and honor and power; for Thou didst create all things, and because of Thy will they existed, and were created'" (Revelation 4:8,11).

Maybe you would like to join me and enter into His gates with praise and into His courts with thanksgiving—giving thanks to Him for our "so great" salvation. Why don't you do it now, Beloved?

— D A Y   F O U R —

Having been cleansed by the blood of Jesus Christ from an evil conscience, how do you *stay* pure? How do you keep your heart from being stained all over again?

The first thing I want you to see is that you keep your heart cleansed through the Word of God. When the Word cleanses us, it cleanses from wrong thinking, wrong doctrine, and wrong behavior. Read carefully the following two passages, printed out below. Watch for and mark the word *sanctify.* Then notice what is sanctified (set apart, declared holy) and how it is accomplished.

◗ EPHESIANS 5:25-26

25 Husbands, love your wives, just as Christ also loved the church and gave Himself up for her;

26 that He might sanctify her, having cleansed her by the washing of water with the word.

◗ JOHN 17:17

Sanctify them in the truth; Thy word is truth.

The word *sanctify* has the same basic root as the word *holy*, and it means either "holy" or "set apart."

1. According to these two verses, how are you made holy? How are you kept clean?

2. How often do you think such cleansing is necessary? How much do you think it takes to make or keep you clean?

I have heard some people say, "Just spend three minutes a day alone with God."

I can understand, I think, where they're coming from. Some believers go through their days without spending any time with the Lord. And three minutes with God is better than none!

But the question is, "Are we selling God short? Are we selling God's Word short?" Is Deuteronomy 8:3 true when it says that "man does not live by bread alone, but man lives by everything that proceeds out of the mouth of the LORD"? Was Paul a fool for laying down his life in order to declare to others the whole counsel of God? Is the Word of God truly "profitable for teaching, for reproof, for correction, for training in righteousness; that the man of God may be adequate, equipped for every good work" (2 Timothy 3:16-17)? In three minutes a day can I really present myself "approved to God as a workman who does not need to be ashamed, handling accurately the word of truth" (2 Timothy 2:15)?

Why do we look around us and see so many messed up lives? I believe it is because we have not esteemed God's Word as more precious than our necessary food. We have not known His Word so that it has become a light to our feet and a lamp to our paths. Therefore, we have walked in darkness and have stumbled.

I have been amazed, appalled, and grieved at the number of people who come to me after I have spoken and say, "But, Kay, I just didn't *know* these things. I didn't *know* that's what God's Word said. I didn't realize I was going against the will of God!"

So many have been conformed to the world instead of being transformed by the renewing of their minds. That's why lives, homes, and relationships are in such tragic disarray.

Do you see why I am so thankful to God for people like you? You are giving yourself to a study of God's Word. You are seeking the whole counsel of God. And He has promised to meet your seeking heart!

Devoted time in God's Word is vital if you're going to have a pure heart. Take a moment now and settle this issue with God. Talk to Him about it. But before you do, let me give you one more insight.

Your heart is also kept cleansed and made pure through confession. The Bible tells us that "if we confess our sins, He is faithful and righteous to forgive us our sins and to cleanse us from all unrighteousness" (1 John 1:9). *Confess* means to "say the same thing" or to "speak the same word." Therefore, to confess our sins is to agree with God that what we have done is sin. To do that we name it as sin. We say, "God, I have permitted _____ to rule me, and that is sin. I confess it as sin right now. I want to turn from that sin."

When we do this, we have a marvelous promise. Because God is faithful and because He is righteous, He forgives our sin. He looks at that blood of Jesus on the Mercy Seat, the blood that cleanses us from sin.

He also cleanses us from "all unrighteousness." Have you ever wondered where you would stand with God if you hadn't confessed some sin because you couldn't remember it? First John 1:9 promises you that when you confess every known sin, then God cleanses you from all unrighteousness. Why? Because as I told you earlier in this study, God sees a heart that *wants* to be pure, and so moves accordingly.

Isn't it wonderful to be pure?

The reason so many people can't really see God and don't have an intimate relationship with Him is because their hearts are so defiled. They are so filled with the filth and muck of this world that they have no spiritual sensitivity. That is why it is vital that you spend time being made clean every single day. Stand in the holy shower of God's Word, and scrub yourself from head to toe. Get rid of the stench of this world. It will transform you. Your life will be a sweet fragrance in the nostrils of God.

Think about these things, Beloved. Talk to God about them. Do business with Him. If you have neglected His Word, then you need to confess that and get into the habit of going through God's Word consistently. Studying books such as this one can help you, but you must also make sure that you *read* through God's Word consistently. Let's talk more about that tomorrow.

— D A Y   F I V E —

Confession helps you keep your heart pure before God. But if you want your heart to be totally cleansed so that nothing stands between you and God, or you and others, then restitution may be necessary.

Does your heart sometimes condemn you?

Have you wronged others in the past, and do you still feel the weight of those wrongs on your conscience?

If your answer is yes to either of these questions, then it's probable you need to make some restitution. Please don't let that thought panic you! I promise you that it's one of the most freeing actions you could ever take.

Let me take you to a passage in the thirty-third chapter of Ezekiel. God is about to destroy Jerusalem and allow His people to be taken into captivity in Babylon. The chapter makes reference to God's approaching judgment on the southern kingdom of Judah because of their grievous sin as a nation. In the beginning of the chapter, Ezekiel is told to warn the people of God's impending judgment. Yet they are also to know God's heart as expressed in Ezekiel 33:11:

> "Say to them, 'As I live!' declares the Lord GOD, 'I take no pleasure in the death of the wicked, but rather that the wicked turn from his way and live. Turn back, turn back from your evil ways! Why then will you die, O house of Israel?'"

Now let's look at some additional verses in this chapter.

● EZEKIEL 33:14-16

14 "But when I say to the wicked, 'You will surely die,' and he turns from his sin and practices justice and righteousness,

15 if a wicked man restores a pledge, pays back what he has taken by robbery, walks by the statutes which ensure life without committing iniquity, he will surely live; he shall not die.

16 "None of his sins that he has committed will be remembered against him. He has practiced justice and righteousness; he will surely live."

When you read the Scriptures, you should continuously ask yourself the 5 W's and H: *Who? What? When? Where? Why?* and *How?* Let's practice this study technique together, referring to the last Ezekiel passage.

1. To WHOM is God speaking?

2. WHAT is going to happen to this man?

3. HOW can it be prevented?

Did you note the list of things that the wicked man may perform so that he will live and not die? Not only will he live, but none of his sins will be remembered against him because to do these things is to practice "justice and righteousness."

Observation is the most valuable and essential part of Bible study, and yet it is usually the most neglected because people don't know how to do it. Part of observing Scripture is looking for lists in the text. Let me show you the one you just observed in the Ezekiel passage and how you could mark it in your Bible.

God gives a list of things that this man should do if he wants to live. The first one is to turn from his sin. So, above "turns from his sin," write a little "1" and circle it. Second, he is to practice justice, so put a "2" above "practices justice." Third, he is to practice righteousness, so put a "3" above "practices righteousness." Fourth, he is to restore a pledge. Put a "4" above "restore a pledge." Fifth, he is to pay back what he has taken by robbery, so put a "5" above that. And sixth, he is to walk by the statutes which ensure life. In other words, he is to walk in obedience to God's Word and not sin. Put your "6" above "walks by the statutes."

Now, back to the question. How is this man going to keep from dying? He is going to keep from dying by doing these things you have marked. These actions demonstrate his desire for a pure heart. He has practiced justice and righteousness. Did you note the two references in this passage to "restitution"? Before we move on, let's take a closer look at this matter.

He first mentions restoring a pledge. Suppose I wanted to buy a piece of property from you but didn't have the money. So I said to you, "Look, I don't have the money, but I want to buy it. Let me give you a hundred dollars as a pledge that I'm going to buy this property." Well, three weeks later I come back and say, "There's no way I can buy it. I just can't get the money together, and I'm in desperate straits."

What are you to do at that point? Will you just cluck your tongue and say, "Tch, tch. That's just too bad. You kept me from selling my property so the hundred dollars is mine!" No, that's what the world would do. The world would take advantage of this situation. But we are not to be like the world. We are to *restore* a pledge.

The second means of restitution referred to in this passage is paying back what has been taken by robbery. Many people who have sat under this teaching have told me that they have been convicted by the Lord because they had not been honest in their dealings with others. Some have actually stolen. Others have cheated on exams in school or bought things they knew were stolen. Because these people went to God seeking a pure heart, God reminded them of these unrighteous dealings. What about you, Beloved? Do you need to make restitution? (If you want to understand more about restitution, read Leviticus 6:1-5.)

Now let me anticipate a question. "But if I ask God to forgive me, isn't that enough?" It would be if you had only sinned against God! But it is not enough if you have stolen something or extorted funds or not returned what was borrowed or cheated on your income tax. Confession is not enough. Those people whom you have sinned against don't know that you have asked God to forgive you. And even if they did, they would say, "What difference does that make to me? I'm still out what you stole from me."

O Beloved, if you want to have a pure heart, then you must make restitution. And when you do, God will not mention your sins to you anymore because you have done what is just and right. If they are being mentioned to you, then you can know it is the devil reminding you rather than God, because you have done what is right in the eyes of God.

Before we move on, let's summarize what we have seen about purity of heart. First, it begins with God's giving us a new heart when we are born again. Then, a pure heart is maintained by staying in the Word of God, where we are washed by the water of the Word. As we do this, we see that a pure heart is a heart that is right before God *and before man.* This is where restitution comes into the picture.

If you're going to have a pure heart, you not only need to make restitution to those you have defrauded, you also need to keep your heart cleansed by carefully watching what you think about. Every thought needs to meet the qualifications of Philippians 4:8:

> Finally, brethren, whatever is true, whatever is honorable, whatever is right, whatever is pure, whatever is lovely, whatever is of good repute, if there is any excellence and if anything worthy of praise, let your mind dwell on these things.

Look carefully at that verse, and then list what kinds of things you are to think upon. (By the way, this is another list you can number right in your Bible.)

The things that you allow to possess your imagination can also get you into serious trouble. When you entertain wrong thoughts, they can eventually become footholds or strongholds for Satan. Second Corinthians 10:5 says: "We are destroying speculations and every lofty thing raised up against the knowledge of God, and we are taking every thought captive to the obedience of Christ."

In your own words, write down God's instructions to you from this verse.

Please also remember the point we made earlier in this study: You need not only to guard your thoughts, but you must also guard the company you keep. One can impact the other! Earlier, we looked at 1 Corinthians 15:33, which says: "Do not be deceived: 'Bad company corrupts good morals.'" God clearly warns us not to walk in the counsel of the wicked, nor stand in the path of sinners, nor sit in the seat of scoffers (see Psalm 1). When we do, we become like them, and our hearts become contaminated. One bad apple is not made good by a bushel of good apples! Instead, the one bad apple will eventually ruin the whole bunch.

Finally, if you are going to have a pure heart and see God, according to James 4:8 you need to purify your heart and not be double-minded. How do you purify your heart? Colossians 3:2 says, "Set your mind on the things above, not on the things that are on earth."

I would like to leave you with a very sobering verse to meditate upon from the book of Hebrews.

> Pursue peace with all men, and the sanctification without which no one will see the Lord. (Hebrews 12:14)

Why does God tell us that we are to pursue sanctification, or holiness? Because without it, no one will see the Lord!
What are you pursuing, Beloved?
Will you see God?

MEMORY VERSE

Blessed are the merciful, for they shall receive mercy.
Blessed are the pure in heart, for they shall see God.

MATTHEW 5:7-8

SMALL-GROUP DISCUSSION QUESTIONS

1. How would you define mercy?
2. How does God display His mercy?
3. How did the tabernacle show God's mercy? What function did the Ark of the Covenant and the Mercy Seat have on the Day of Atonement? What did these foreshadow?
4. Look again at Matthew 18:21-35.
   a. How did the debts of the two men compare?
   b. What was Jesus' purpose in telling this story?
   c. What significance does this story have for our lives?
   d. How did God speak to you personally?
5. Is there anyone you are having a hard time forgiving? If so, take time to pray for that person. Is there someone who could pray with you, perhaps someone who has been in a similar situation?
6. What does it mean to be pure in heart?
7. How does a person get a pure heart?
8. What practical things can we do to keep our hearts pure?
9. What does Ezekiel 33:14-16 tell us will keep a man from dying as a result of God's judgment?
10. Ask the class, "Do any of you need to make restitution for something? If so, can we pray for you or help you in the process?"
11. If you make any necessary restitution, how do you think it will affect your relationship with your heavenly Father? When were you reconciled to God, and what changes have you seen in your life as a result?

PEACEMAKERS...
BUT PERSECUTED

— D A Y O N E —

You've heard it said over and over by desperate men and women in hard situations...even by people on the street. When asked what they want more than anything else, unanimously they say, "Peace."

They don't ask for wealth or fame.

Their only request is peace.

We weren't born for conflict, were we? *"All I want is a little peace!"* It has been shouted, sobbed, screamed, and spit through clenched teeth. Maybe you have said it. I remember times when I have said it. I said it in an unhappy marriage, before I knew Jesus. In a typical mother's anger I have said it to my sons. I have said it when the pressures and responsibilities of ministry have poured in like a flood, leaving me no time to collect my thoughts or "come up for air."

How would you like to have not only peace...but genuine, God-given happiness as well? How would you like to have a peace that does not waver with the wind of circumstances? It's all wrapped up in the seventh beatitude: "Blessed are the peacemakers, for they shall be called sons of God" (Matthew 5:9).

But notice the beatitude which follows: "Blessed are those who have been persecuted."

It doesn't seem to fit, does it? Peacemakers—but persecuted? Yet that is just what Scripture says, and that is what we are going to consider in our study and prayer times together this week. How do peacemakers live? What are they anyway? And why are they called "sons of God"? Then we are going to look at how this dual calling of making peace and enduring persecution fits together.

Peace is a very important word in the Bible. It appears in every New Testament book except 1 John. There are over four hundred references to peace in the Bible.

The Greek word for peace signifies a harmonious relationship. This is important because it shows that peace is not merely the absence of war; peace is harmony. It's not a "cold war." It's not "an uneasy truce." It's not two frowning parties sitting back to back with their arms folded in stony silence. No, peace signifies a willingness to turn toward each other and embrace one another—in spite of differences of opinion.

That is harmony. And, oh, how we need harmony! How we need peace! You and I weren't born for conflict. It takes a terrible toll on mind and body.

We hear a lot of chatter about peace in our world today. But the problem lies deeper than an outward expression. The problem lies with our unseen motives. We are seeking peace, but we want it for ourselves, on our own terms. We want peace horizontally—with mankind. But we cannot have peace because we do not have it *vertically*. There will be no true peace among men until there is true peace with God. Do you know why? Let's examine a few verses that give us some insights. Read the following verses that are printed out for you, and mark every occurrence of the word *heart* with a ♡. Then answer the questions that follow.

▶ GENESIS 8:21

And the LORD smelled the soothing aroma; and the LORD said to

Himself, "I will never again curse the ground on account of man, for the

intent of man's heart is evil from his youth; and I will never again destroy

every living thing, as I have done."

▶ JEREMIAH 17:9

The heart is more deceitful than all else

And is desperately sick;

Who can understand it?

Which parts of these two verses give us a clue as to why there is so little peace among human beings in our world?

What insight does this passage give us regarding humanity's problem with peace?

Which beatitude precedes today's verse about "peacemakers"? Write it out below.

At this point you might find yourself wondering, *How could I ever be pure in heart if my heart is "deceitful and desperately wicked,"* as the *King James Version* says? That's a good question...and it deserves a careful answer. In Ezekiel 36:26-27, God speaks to Israel and Judah concerning fulfillment of the New Covenant. Listen to this wonderful promise:

> Moreover, I will give you a new heart and put a new spirit within you; and I will remove the heart of stone from your flesh and give you a heart of flesh. And I will put My Spirit within you and cause you to walk in My statutes, and you will be careful to observe My ordinances.

The new heart comes with the gift of the Holy Spirit. This is substantiated in 2 Corinthians 3:3, where we read:

> You are a letter of Christ, cared for by us, written not with ink, but with the Spirit of the living God, not on tablets of stone, but on tablets of human hearts.

We have no peace on earth among men because of our wicked human hearts. But—praise God—He has given a much-needed "heart transplant" to all who have turned to Him for salvation!

Now, having discussed this matter of the heart, do you know where true peace originates? By now you should know that the answer is Jesus. You say, "Yes, but I thought He was to bring peace on earth. Isn't that what the angels said? 'Peace on earth…good will'? What happened? Where's the peace?"

These are good questions. Let's do further research.

Read the passages that follow, and underline each occurence of the word *peace.*

❶ ISAIAH 9:6

> For a child will be born to us, a son will be given to us;
>
> And the government will rest on His shoulders;

And His name will be called Wonderful Counselor, Mighty God,

Eternal Father, Prince of Peace.

This passage is a prophecy about the Lord Jesus Christ. Which of Jesus' titles pertains to our lesson?

▶ LUKE 2:13-14

13 And suddenly there appeared with the angel a multitude of the heavenly host praising God, and saying,

14 "Glory to God in the highest,

And on earth peace among men with whom He is pleased."

Does this passage actually say that Jesus is going to bring peace on earth? What *does* it say?

▶ LUKE 12:51-53

51 "Do you suppose that I came to grant peace on earth? I tell you, no, but rather division;

52 for from now on five members in one household will be divided, three against two, and two against three.

53 "They will be divided, father against son, and son against father; mother against daughter, and daughter against mother; mother-in-law against daughter-in-law, and daughter-in-law against mother-in-law."

In your own words, write out what Jesus is saying regarding peace.

 JOHN 14:27

Peace I leave with you; My peace I give to you; not as the world gives, do I give to you. Let not your heart be troubled, nor let it be fearful.

Once again, rewrite this verse in your own words.

Jesus did come to bring peace—but a different kind of peace than what the world talks about. When the United Nations was instituted in 1945, its motto spoke of sparing succeeding generations from the scourge of war. Yet there has not been a day of peace since 1945.

Peace on earth? It will not happen until Jesus returns to reign as King of kings. Even then, it will be an enforced peace, for Jesus will rule with a rod of iron. Why? Because even at that time, all men's hearts will not be right toward God. According to a literal interpretation of Revelation 20, at the end of Jesus' thousand-year reign, Satan will be loosed from the bottomless pit to gather out of Jesus' kingdom all who still resist the lordship of Jesus Christ.

A fearsome battle will follow—the battle of Gog and Magog. Then God will destroy this earth by fire and create a new heaven and a new earth. Then and only then will there be true peace.

"But Kay," you may wonder, "do I have to wait that long?"

No, Beloved. Jesus came that you might have peace *right now*—no matter what your circumstances are. We'll discuss it more tomorrow. Today think about the things you have learned. Take time to talk to God about them in honest, open prayer. Ask Him questions, and He will give you answers.

He always has time for you.

– D A Y   T W O –

"Blessed are the peacemakers, for they shall be called sons of God" (Matthew 5:9).

What makes a peacemaker?

First, if I'm going to be a peacemaker, I must be at peace with God.

Sinners are at enmity with God. Enmity is a state of disharmony, the feeling that enemies have for one another. It is hatred, hostility, or animosity. Therefore, reconciliation is necessary. To reconcile means "to take two who were separated from one another because of enmity and to bring them back into oneness or harmony."

Man separated himself from God. It is God who has sought to reconcile man to Himself. When man moved away from God because of his sin, God in His love moved toward man to bring him back to Himself. How did He do it?

Read Colossians 1:19-22, printed below.

▶ COLOSSIANS 1:19-22

19 For it was the Father's good pleasure for all the fulness to dwell in Him,

20 and through Him to reconcile all things to Himself, having made peace through the blood of His cross; through Him, I say, whether things on earth or things in heaven.

21 And although you were formerly alienated and hostile in mind, engaged in evil deeds, yet He has now reconciled you in His fleshly body through death, in order to present you before Him holy and blameless and beyond reproach—

Circle the words *peace* and *reconcile* in this passage, and then answer the following questions:

1. Who did the reconciling?

2. What was the state of man when he was being reconciled?

3. How were the reconciliation and peace made possible?

Now read Romans 5:10-11 and mark every reference to *reconcile* or *reconciliation*. Then answer the questions which follow.

▶ ROMANS 5:10-11

10 For if while we were enemies, we were reconciled to God through the death of His Son, much more, having been reconciled, we shall be saved by His life.

11 And not only this, but we also exult in God through our Lord Jesus Christ, through whom we have now received the reconciliation.

1. What were we when God reconciled us to Himself?

2. How were we reconciled to God?

3. Through whom did we receive the reconciliation?

Now...what have you seen? If you are going to be a peacemaker, you must first have peace with God. Jesus is the Prince of Peace, the Child that was born to die so that you, an enemy of God, might be reconciled through the death of His Son. Jesus is God's Peace Child.

Have you read Don Richardson's book *Peace Child?* What a gripping story! Don Richardson and his wife were missionaries among the Sawi people, headhunting cannibals of Netherlands New Guinea. The members of this tribe pillowed their heads each night on the skulls of their victims. With them, treachery was more than a way of life. It was an *ideal.* They reveled in treachery! Because of this they lived in constant conflict. Sawi villages constantly fought among themselves. Peace seemed impossible.

Finally, unable to bear all the bloodshed and death, Richardson (known to the people as "Tuan") approached them and told them that if they did not make peace, he would leave them. The people were panic-stricken. How could Tuan leave them? In desperation the men met and then approached Don. They promised: "Tuan, tomorrow we are going to make peace!"

Peace! How could a people who prized treachery above all else make peace with anyone—let alone their sworn, blood enemies? Little did the missionary realize that the following day's ceremony would be a key to unlock the Sawi's spiritual darkness and captivity. According to tribal laws, there would never be peace until a "peace child" was given to the enemy.

You must read this book! The story will tear at your heart as you see a mother screaming, struggling to break free of those restraining her, crying, "No! No! He's our only son." Her husband, clutching their son in his arms, continued to walk resolutely into the camp of the enemy. Peace had to be made, no matter the cost.

> Kaiyo's chest was heaving with emotion as he reached the edge of Haenam. The leading men of the village were massed in front of him now, expectantly eyeing the child Kaiyo held in his hands. Kaiyo scanned the row of enemy faces before him.... Then he saw the man he had chosen and called his name. "Mahor!" he cried.
>
> "Mahor!" Kaiyo challenged. "Will you plead the words of Kamur among your people?"
>
> "Yes!" Mahor responded, "I will plead the words of Kamur among my people!"
>
> "Then I give you my son and with him my name!"
>
> Mahor shouted, "Eehaa! It is enough! I will surely plead for peace between us!..."
>
> Suddenly Mahaen reappeared in the forefront of the crowd. Facing Kaiyo, Mahaen held aloft one of his other baby sons and cried, "Kaiyo! Will you plead the words of Haenam among your people?"
>
> "Yes!" cried Kaiyo, holding out his hands toward Mahaen.
>
> "Then I will give you my son and with him my name!"[1]

They had exchanged sons and they had exchanged names. Richardson did not understand.

> "Why is this necessary?" [he] asked.
>
> "Tuan, you've been urging us to make peace—don't you know it's impossible to have peace without a peace child?"[2]

Oh, Beloved, don't you know that it's impossible for you to have peace without a peace child? God left heaven and came into the enemy's camp. He brought you His only Son and said, "Peace among those with whom God is well-pleased." God is well-pleased with those who come to

Him in poverty of spirit, confessing that they are sinners and accepting God's Peace Child.

Do you have God's Peace Child? Without Him, you'll never be a son or daughter of God.

Without Him, you'll never be a peacemaker. Without Him, your heart will always be deceitful, desperately wicked. Only Jesus can give you a new heart.

– D A Y   T H R E E –

What makes you a peacemaker?

First, it is having peace with God. Secondly, it's having peace with the body of Jesus Christ. Ephesians 4:1-3 tells us very clearly that if we are to walk "in a manner worthy of the calling with which you have been called," we must be "diligent to preserve the unity of the Spirit in the bond of peace."

Read the following passages. Underline the words *peace* and/or *reconciled.* Then answer the questions that follow.

▶ 1 THESSALONIANS 5:12-13

12 But we request of you, brethren, that you appreciate those who diligently labor among you, and have charge over you in the Lord and give you instruction,

13 and that you esteem them very highly in love because of their work. Live in peace with one another.

What does this passage say about peace? (Before you answer that, let me tell you about the verb *live.* In the last sentence of the verse, *live* is a present tense, imperative active verb, which indicates continuous or habitual action. The imperative mood is a command, and the active voice indicates the subject does the action of the verb.) Now then, what is God's word to His people regarding peace?

▶ MATTHEW 5:22-24

22 "But I say to you that everyone who is angry with his brother shall be guilty before the court; and whoever shall say to his brother, 'Raca,' shall be guilty before the supreme court; and whoever shall say, 'You fool,' shall be guilty enough to go into the fiery hell.

23 "If therefore you are presenting your offering at the altar, and there remember that your brother has something against you,

24 leave your offering there before the altar, and go your way; first be reconciled to your brother, and then come and present your offering."

1. When it says "be reconciled to your brother," do you think He is talking about a literal blood brother? Explain your answer.

2. Who is to go to whom? Why?

3. How do you think this agrees with 1 Thessalonians 5:13?

What is God telling us in these verses? Isn't He saying that if we are going to be obedient to Him, we have a responsibility to live in peace with one another? If we know that a brother or sister in Christ has something against us, we are responsible, as peacemakers, to go to that offended individual and make peace. Blessed—or spiritually prosperous—are the peacemakers! Are you blessed of God because you are making and keeping peace in the body?

A third thing that makes you a peacemaker is having the ministry of reconciliation. A key element of peacemaking is bringing the gospel of peace to other people so that they in turn might have peace with God. You and I are not only to make peace among ourselves, we are to make peace with those who are outside Christ. There is really only one way to do that: Introduce them to the Prince of Peace.

Read the following passage and mark every reference to *reconciliation*. Then answer the questions which follow.

❿ 2 CORINTHIANS 5:14-21

14 For the love of Christ controls us, having concluded this, that one died for all, therefore all died;

15 and He died for all, that they who live should no longer live for themselves, but for Him who died and rose again on their behalf.

16 Therefore from now on we recognize no man according to the flesh; even though we have known Christ according to the flesh, yet now we know Him thus no longer.

17 Therefore if any man is in Christ, he is a new creature; the old things passed away; behold, new things have come.

18 Now all these things are from God, who reconciled us to Himself through Christ, and gave us the ministry of reconciliation,

19 namely, that God was in Christ reconciling the world to Himself, not counting their trespasses against them, and He has committed to us the word of reconciliation.

20 Therefore, we are ambassadors for Christ, as though God were entreating through us; we beg you on behalf of Christ, be reconciled to God.

21 He made Him who knew no sin to be sin on our behalf, that we might become the righteousness of God in Him.

1. According to verses 14-15, for whom did Jesus die?

2. Because He died for us, for whom are we to live?

3. To whom has God given a ministry? What kind of ministry is it?

Ambassadors for Christ—that is what you and I are to be!

But are we?

If not...can we really call ourselves peacemakers?

God has given every child of God the ministry of reconciliation. He has committed to you the word of reconciliation, the gospel of Jesus Christ. Isaiah 52:7 says, "How lovely on the mountains are the feet of him who brings good news, who announces peace and brings good news of happiness, who announces salvation." The glad tidings of good things is the gospel of Jesus Christ which brings forgiveness of sins.

Look at your feet. Are they lovely in the eyes of God? Jesus' feet were nailed to a cross so that your feet might someday walk streets of gold. Are you going to walk them alone? Or will others walk beside you—others with whom you have shared the good news so that they, too, might know how to have peace with God?

"But it's hard! I don't know what to say! I get so embarrassed!"

I know that it's hard and that it's difficult to know what to say. But those are not adequate excuses. Jesus said, "Go...and lo, I am with you always" (Matthew 28:19-20). Give Him your mouth, and He will give you His words! Be willing to be made a fool for Christ's sake, and He will make you an ambassador for the world's sake.

I have found myself in all sorts of frightening, awkward situations—situations I would have gladly retreated from except for one fact: How are people going to believe in someone of whom they have never heard? And how are they going to hear unless and until someone tells them? (See Romans 10:14.) You and I are not to be "ashamed of the gospel, for it is the power of God for salvation to everyone who believes, to the Jew first and also to the Greek" (Romans 1:16).

A number of years ago I found myself staying in the same hotel as the actor John Wayne. "The Duke" had always been one of my favorite actors. So when I found myself in an elevator with him and several other people one morning, I was absolutely speechless. Later, as he walked through the hotel lobby with that famous stride of his, people gawked. Others sought his autograph. As I watched, God spoke to my heart, and I knew that I was to share the gospel with him. I thought my heart was literally going to bounce out of my chest and roll around on that marble lobby floor. I felt as weak as a kitten, and if I had delayed right then in order to argue with the Lord, I would have missed the opportunity forever.

I managed to follow him out through the hotel door. And there he was, standing a few yards away from me, waiting for a cab. I was terribly nervous, but I swallowed my fear and walked over to him.

"Mr. Wayne, please excuse me. I've noticed that everyone seems to want something *from* you—asking for your autograph or whatever. But all I want to do is share Someone *with* you. Someone who has drastically changed my life."

With that I handed him a little gospel tract, which he politely accepted. My attempt was not polished, to say the least. I felt like a fool before man, but I had been obedient to God.

You know, Beloved, when I heard that The Duke had died, I was so thankful I had been obedient. I knew that John Wayne's blood would never be upon my hands. Paul wrote, "Therefore I testify to you this day, that I am innocent of the blood of all men. For I did not shrink from declaring to you the whole purpose of God" (Acts 20:26-27).

Are you a peacemaker? Do you have peace with God? Do you seek to keep the unity of the Spirit in the bond of peace? Are you sharing the gospel of peace with others? If so, you will be called a son of God. Like Father, like son! Isn't it wonderful?

— D A Y   F O U R —

Peacemakers, but persecuted!

To those who don't understand spiritual things, the two don't seem to fit. Yet those who are familiar with Jesus' sojourn here on earth know that it describes the life of the Prince of Peace. For "He came to His own, and those who were His own did not receive Him" (John 1:11). Instead they plotted against Him to take His life. They would not have this man to rule over them! He was light in the midst of darkness, but men preferred darkness rather than light because their deeds were evil. So they sought to put out the Light. He was of the truth, but they were of their father, the devil. And they wanted to do the desires of their father, the father of lies. So they crucified Truth.

Jesus warned His disciples:

"Remember the word that I said to you, 'A slave is not greater than his master.' If they persecuted Me, they will also persecute you; if they kept My word, they will keep yours also. But all these things they will do to you for My name's sake, because they do not know the One who sent Me." (John 15:20-21)

Because of what Jesus was, they persecuted Him.

Because of what Jesus makes you, they will persecute you also.

In this last beatitude, "Blessed are those who have been persecuted for the sake of righteousness…," we clearly see the conflict that results from the character of those first seven beatitudes. Remember our outline of the Sermon on the Mount:

Matthew 5:3-9:

The *Character* of Those Who Belong to the Kingdom of Heaven

Matthew 5:10-12:

The *Conflict* of Those Who Belong to the Kingdom of Heaven

Matthew 5:13–7:27:

The *Conduct* of Those Who Belong to the Kingdom of Heaven

As we have seen, the Sermon on the Mount shows us the righteous lifestyle of those who belong to the kingdom of heaven. Such a lifestyle will inevitably bring persecution because it makes us radically different from the rest of this world, those who walk the broad path that leads to destruction (Matthew 7:13).

I believe that Christians in the United States of America will face an intense period of persecution in the not-too-distant future. My heart's burden and question for you is this: *Are you prepared to handle it?* How I pray that this brief study will whet your appetite to dig deeper into God's Word on this subject. God's Word can prepare you to be "adequate and equipped" for whatever missiles Satan may throw at you in the coming days.

Before we consider further questions regarding persecution and suffering, let's take a closer look together at Matthew 5:10-12. There are two "blesseds" here, and yet I do not believe that there are two separate beatitudes. Both of them refer to a blessedness for those suffering persecution.

Verse 10 says, "Blessed are those who have been persecuted for the sake of righteousness."

"Have been persecuted" is what Greek scholars call the perfect tense and the passive voice. The perfect tense denotes past, completed action with a continuous or ongoing result. The passive voice means that the subject is receiving the action of the verb. In other words, these people have already undergone persecution.

To whom is Jesus referring? Are they different from those He speaks of in verse 11: "Blessed are you when men cast insults at you, and persecute you, and say all kinds of evil against you falsely, on account of Me"?

I believe Jesus had two different audiences in mind. When he said, "Blessed are those who have been persecuted," He could have been referring to those such as John the Baptist, who were already undergoing persecution because of their righteous stand and lifestyle. In verse 11, I believe He is referring to His immediate audience—but the application is to you and me. In these two verses, He is simply uniting those who *have already been and are being* persecuted, and those who *will be* persecuted.

The Sermon on the Mount, you will remember, was delivered in the early days of Jesus' ministry. Persecution was not yet in full bloom. Jesus is saying that whenever a man is persecuted for the sake of righteousness, to whatever degree, he can rejoice. The word for "rejoice and be glad" means to be exceedingly happy. Why? Because (1) his reward in heaven is great (and the word means "exceedingly great!"); (2) he is in the company of the prophets who were persecuted before him. (He has joined the ranks of godly men and women who counted it a privilege to lay down their lives for their God.)

Let's take time to review these verses and allow the truth to take root in our hearts. Read them and mark every reference to *persecution* in any form. Then answer the questions which follow.

◗ MATTHEW 5:10-12

10 Blessed are those who have been persecuted for the sake of righteousness, for theirs is the kingdom of heaven.

11 Blessed are you when men cast insults at you, and persecute you, and say all kinds of evil against you falsely, on account of Me.

12 Rejoice, and be glad, for your reward in heaven is great, for so they persecuted the prophets who were before you.

1. Why are they being persecuted?

2. According to these verses, what form does that persecution take?

3. Are they alone in their persecution?

Now let's look at some things you need to know regarding persecution and suffering.

Suffering is a certainty for every believer because suffering is a confirming sign of your own salvation! Read Philippians 1:27-30, printed out for you, and mark every reference to suffering. Then answer the questions that follow.

▶ PHILIPPIANS 1:27-30

27 Only conduct yourselves in a manner worthy of the gospel of Christ; so that whether I come and see you or remain absent, I may hear of you that you are standing firm in one spirit, with one mind striving together for the faith of the gospel;

28 in no way alarmed by your opponents—which is a sign of destruction for them, but of salvation for you, and that too, from God.

29 For to you it has been granted for Christ's sake, not only to believe in Him, but also to suffer for His sake,

30 experiencing the same conflict which you saw in me, and now hear to be in me.

1. According to verse 29, two things have been granted you for Christ's sake. What are they?

2. According to this passage, how are we to conduct ourselves?

3. What are we to do when we are opposed? How are we to respond to our opponents?

4. What does this type of response demonstrate to our opponents?

5. What does this kind of response demonstrate to us?

Through the apostle Paul, God is telling us that the gift of faith in Christ Jesus and the gift of suffering come together. When you stand before your opponents and you are not alarmed, it becomes a sign of salvation for you. You realize that you have a home in heaven. So even if God permits them to take your life, He is simply saying, "It's time to come on Home, My child."

This sort of attitude alarms your opponents! When they see you standing firm before them without being shaken, it "is a sign of destruction for them." Why? Because they know that if *they* were in your shoes, they would melt with panic! And to you, it becomes a testimony of the reality of your faith!

What insight do these truths give you into presenting the gospel to others or into discipling brand-new Christians? The book of 1 Thessalonians helps answer that question.

The first three chapters of 1 Thessalonians give us an account of what happened when Paul, Silvanus, and Timothy went to Thessalonica to deliver the gospel. In 1 Thessalonians 3:3-4 we discover what Paul taught his new converts. Among other things, he dealt with suffering and told them not to be disturbed by the afflictions that they were facing. Mark the words *suffering* and *affliction* and any pronouns which refer to them.

▶ 1 THESSALONIANS 3:3-4

3 For you yourselves know that we have been destined for this.

4 For indeed when we were with you, we kept telling you in advance that we were going to suffer affliction; and so it came to pass, as you know.

Paul had wisely taught them that suffering and persecution go with salvation. Do we teach this also? Does this form an integral part of our witnessing and discipling?

Isn't this what we see in the Sermon on the Mount? What is the blessedness of those who are persecuted? It's the same as the blessedness of those who are poor in spirit: "theirs is the kingdom of heaven." It is a present-tense possession. The Beatitudes begin and end with the promise, "theirs is the kingdom of heaven." Therefore, everything in between is included. It's a package deal. These Beatitudes become the attributes or character of the child of God, a character that results in conflict. But that conflict becomes the very surety of our salvation!

I don't want to overwhelm you with Scripture at this point (and there won't be any extra credit!), but you could learn a great deal more by looking up and pondering the following verses: 1 Peter 4:1-2,12-16; John 15:18; 16:33; 2 Timothy 3:12.

As you go to the Lord in prayer, remember that there are degrees of persecution. First Peter 4:13 points this out: "But to the degree that you share the sufferings of Christ, keep on rejoicing."

What is God saying here? I think He is saying this:

> the greater the obedience, the greater the righteousness;
> the greater the righteousness, the greater the suffering;
> the greater the suffering, the greater the rejoicing.

O Beloved, are you suffering at all for the gospel of Jesus Christ? Do men and women spurn you, mock you, or drag your name through the mud because of your relationship with the Lord? If not, could it possibly be that you're not all you ought to be for Him? Could it be that you have compromised His standard of righteousness? Are you so like the world that your life does not expose their sin and, therefore, they feel very comfortable with you? Or are you so isolated and insulated in your own little Christian atmosphere that you are too comfortable to step out into the world to be a peacemaker? Have you forgotten that you are an ambassador for Jesus Christ? Have you forgotten that He commissioned you to witness to the lost? Have you refused to go where Jesus said to go because you wanted to avoid the hassles and heartache?

Life speeds by so quickly! You need to examine yourself now...before your life is used up and you have no more days to live for Him who died for you.

– D A Y   F I V E –

Yesterday we saw that suffering is a certainty for the child of God. It is a sign of our salvation. On this last day of our study of Matthew 5:9-12, we will look at several other things we need to know regarding persecution and suffering.

We need to know that suffering prepares us for glory.

That helps, doesn't it? If you and I could grasp the fact that our suffering has an eternal purpose—or any purpose at all—it would be easier to deal with. No one wants to think that his or her grief, sorrow, and troubles are all a waste! Paul gives us this word in the book of Romans:

> The Spirit Himself bears witness with our spirit that we are children of God, and if children, heirs also, heirs of God and fellow heirs with Christ, if indeed we suffer with Him in order that we may also be glorified with Him. (Romans 8:16-17)

When it says, "if indeed we suffer with *Him,*" the *if* means *since* "we suffer with Him." In other words, suffering is a mark of our family relationship with God the Father and the Lord Jesus Christ. But we see another truth as well. Suffering is *necessary* in order that we may be glorified with Him.

How does suffering prepare us for glory? Suffering gets rid of the dross in our lives; it is God's crucible of purification. With this in mind, read the verses below and mark every reference to trials or testing:

▶ 1 P E T E R 1 : 6 - 7

⁶ In this you greatly rejoice, even though now for a little while, if necessary, you have been distressed by various trials,

⁷ that the proof of your faith, being more precious than gold which is

perishable, even though tested by fire, may be found to result in praise and glory and honor at the revelation of Jesus Christ.

Do you know what I mean when I speak of "God's crucible of purification"? It's a word picture drawn from the ancient art of the mining and purification of silver. When silver is first extracted from the earth, it is tainted by various impurities. Purification occurs in a crucible over a hot flame. The process of heating the metal to a molten state and skimming off the impurities may be repeated as often as seven times, with each purifying fire more intense than the last. In this way, the metal finally yields the last of its impurities, leaving pure silver behind.

During the purification process, the silversmith skims off the dross that floats to the top of the liquid silver. Looking into the smooth pool of molten metal, the craftsman searches for his own reflected image on the surface. At first the image is very dim, and he knows that impurities remain. So he builds the fire to an even greater intensity. He never leaves the crucible unattended but hovers beside it, watching it closely. He repeats the process over and over until, finally, he can see a clear and perfect image of himself. When the silver becomes a mirror, he knows it is pure.

This, Beloved, is how suffering and persecution prepare us for glory. It is a fire God uses to consume the dross of our lives so that we finally reflect a clear and perfect image of Him.

In an earlier generation Haralan Popov wrote of this process in a land where communism sought to terrorize believers and destroy the Christian faith.

As the fires of persecution grew, they burned away the chaff and stubble and left only the golden wheat. The suffering purified the church and united the believers in a wonderful spirit of brotherly love such as must have existed in the early church. Petty differences were put aside. Brethren loved and cared for one another and carried one another's burdens. There were no nominal or "lukewarm" believers. It made no sense to be a halfhearted Christian when the price for faith was so great. There came a great spiritual depth and richness in Christ I had never seen in the times before when we were free. Every man, woman, and youth was forced to "count the cost" and decide if serving Christ was worth the suffering. And to the Communists' great regret, this was the healthiest thing they could have done for the church, for the insincere gave up but the true Christians became aware of what Christ meant to them and became more dedicated than ever before.[3]

Even Old Testament saints recognized that suffering prepared them for glory. Hebrews 11:35 reports that "others were tortured, not accepting their release, in order that they might obtain a better resurrection." O Beloved, do not run away from suffering. You can know with certainty that it is to prepare you for glory and for a better resurrection.

Since suffering is certain, it is vital that we know how to respond in our suffering. As we have already seen in Matthew 5:12 and 1 Peter 1:6, we are to rejoice! But how are we to respond to those who have *caused* our suffering? This is answered for us in 1 Peter, which has much to say about suffering and glory. Read 1 Peter 2:18-25, and mark every occurrence of the words *suffer, suffering,* and *suffered.* (You might want to underline them with a red squiggly line.) Then answer the questions that follow.

▶ 1 PETER 2:18-25

18 Servants, be submissive to your masters with all respect, not only to those who are good and gentle, but also to those who are unreasonable.

19 For this finds favor, if for the sake of conscience toward God a man bears up under sorrows when suffering unjustly.

20 For what credit is there if, when you sin and are harshly treated, you endure it with patience? But if when you do what is right and suffer for it you patiently endure it, this finds favor with God.

21 For you have been called for this purpose, since Christ also suffered for you, leaving you an example for you to follow in His steps,

22 WHO COMMITTED NO SIN, NOR WAS ANY DECEIT FOUND IN HIS MOUTH;

23 and while being reviled, He did not revile in return; while suffering, He uttered no threats, but kept entrusting Himself to Him who judges righteously;

24 and He Himself bore our sins in His body on the cross, that we might die to sin and live to righteousness; for by His wounds you were healed.

25 For you were continually straying like sheep, but now you have returned to the Shepherd and Guardian of your souls.

1. What kind of suffering finds favor with God? In other words, which type of suffering is a just suffering?

2. Who is our example in suffering?

3. Note below the specific things Jesus did when He was suffering. Be brief but explicit in your answer.

Jesus is our Example. We are to follow in His steps. This Greek word for *example—hypogrammos—*means "an outline, a drawing, or a copy-book of letters to be used by the pupil." It is used only here in the New Testament. In 1 Peter 2:21-25, Peter gives us a pattern to follow when we suffer.

First, when Jesus suffered, He did not sin. Many times suffering tempts us to react in a fleshly way and to walk independently of God. In the very midst of our suffering, then, we need to cry out to God and cast ourselves upon Him. He will help us to hold our fleshly reflexes in check.

Second, we see that Jesus kept His mouth shut. He uttered no threats. No deceit was found in His mouth. He didn't revile when they reviled Him. He didn't say, "You're going to get yours later!" In the midst of persecution, it's a temptation to retaliate with our mouths, isn't it?

Third, Jesus prayed. He stayed in communion with God. He "kept entrusting Himself to Him who judges righteously" (1 Peter 2:23).

Fourth, He not only prayed, He trusted in His Father, the One who would righteously judge His tormentors. O Beloved, one of the benefits of persecution is intimate communion with the Father and the Son. The Father and the Son know, they understand. Your Father is the God of all comfort, but He can comfort only those who stay in communion with Him. His arms are always opened wide, but you must run into them.

Last of all, Jesus took the persecution. He bore our sins in His body. As we saw, the verb in Matthew 5:10 for "have been persecuted" is in the passive voice; those referred to received the persecution. They did not flee from it. They were willing to endure.

You are not to fear, my friend, no matter what persecution or suffering comes into your life.

God is sovereign.

He is in control.

God holds you in His hand (John 10:28-30), and God is love. Therefore, you can know with certainty that whatever touches your life has first been filtered through fingers of love. Because of that, you can bear it—or He would never have permitted it. And in the bearing of it, you will testify to the reality of your faith in Jesus Christ. You, like Christ, may actually bring others into His eternal kingdom through your suffering.

Finally, you must know your responsibility to those who are suffering. Hebrews 13:3 says, "Remember the prisoners, as though in prison with them, and those who are ill-treated, since you yourselves also are in the body."4

We are to suffer with those who suffer. We are not to stand on the sidelines and allow others to suffer alone. We are not to be ashamed of the testimony of our Lord, or of His prisoners, but we are to "join with [*them*] in suffering for the gospel according to the power of God" (2 Timothy 1:8).

Peacemakers...and the persecuted.

The two really do go together.

May the longing of your heart be to "know Him, and the power of His resurrection and the fellowship of His sufferings" (Philippians 3:10). And may we never forget Jesus' words of warning, "Woe to you when all men speak well of you, for in the same way their fathers used to treat the false prophets" (Luke 6:26).

MEMORY VERSE

Blessed are the peacemakers, for they shall be called sons of God. Blessed are those who have been persecuted for the sake of righteousness, for theirs is the kingdom of heaven. Blessed are you when men cast insults at you, and persecute you, and say all kinds of evil against you falsely, on account of Me. Rejoice, and be glad, for your reward in heaven is great, for so they persecuted the prophets who were before you.

MATTHEW 5:9-12

SMALL-GROUP DISCUSSION QUESTIONS

1. What is the true meaning of peace?
2. According to Genesis 8:21 and Jeremiah 17:9, why is there no peace among human beings?
3. How do we get a new heart? Have some of the class share how their hearts changed when God saved them.
4. How can people be at peace with each other? Explain the words *enmity* and *reconcile*.
5. How can man be reconciled to God? Look once again at Colossians 1:20-22; Romans 5:10-11, and 2 Corinthians 5:18-21. What do these say about reconciliation?
6. What brings disharmony between believers? What practical things can Christians do to make peace?
7. What part does persecution play in the life of a Christian? Explain your answer using Scripture.
8. What forms can persecution take?
9. What purpose does persecution have?
10. How are we to handle it when persecution comes? What do we learn from Jesus' example in 1 Peter 2:21-25?

11. Ask if anyone is suffering persecution now and how the class can pray for him or her.
12. Have the class review Matthew 5:9-12 or whatever portion they have memorized.

9

SALT, LIGHT, AND YOU

— DAY ONE —

It was December, almost Christmas. The airport was jammed. Our flight had been delayed, impatient travelers milled through the airport gate, and there was no place to sit down.

I stood at the window, watching the airport lights decorate the darkness of night. Blue, red, yellow—to my eyes they were Christmas lights, strung across the runways in honor of Him. My heart was full. I was on my way to Augusta to speak, and it was all because of Him. The Savior. The Son of Man.

My eyes went from the lights on the runway to the heavens above, as I silently communed with my Father. I felt awed by His love. I thought of Jesus, born to die that I who was dead might have life—a life I had longed for but had never really known existed. Oh, how He had changed me.

Suddenly my thoughts were interrupted by a voice behind me.

"Oh *Christ!* That's not the way it was…"

An arrow pierced my heart! Where had it come from? I turned. He was easy to identify because he continued to use the Lord's name in vain. There he stood, a handsome, well-dressed man in his late thirties, in all probability an executive or a salesman. I turned back to the window. I didn't want to hear what he was saying. It hurt.

But I could hear nothing else, and the pressure within me continued to mount. I knew God wanted me to speak to the man. But how? What would I say? How should I approach him? I stalled for time and for composure. My heart was thumping rapidly, and I knew that, upset as I was, my voice would sound high and trembly.

Finally I walked over, smiled, and said, "Excuse me. I couldn't help overhearing your conversation. I know this is presumptuous, but may I ask you a question? Are you going to celebrate Christmas this year?"

He looked at me, a little taken aback but curious.

"Yes," he said, "I am."

"Do you know what Christmas is all about?"

From there I shared Christ and the gravity of taking God's name in vain. His response was interesting. He wanted to talk, to apologize, and to listen.

Salt and light, that's what we are supposed to be.

And if we are not...what then?

Jesus said: "You are the salt of the earth; but if the salt has become tasteless, how will it be made salty again? It is good for nothing anymore, except to be thrown out and trampled under foot by men. You are the light of the world. A city set on a hill cannot be hidden" (Matthew 5:13-14).

Salt and light—two metaphors—following a series of "blesseds." Their purpose is highly significant. Suddenly we see our reason for being. We have worth. We are needed. Our lives can count. The *amount* of salt added to any recipe makes a difference, doesn't it? We know because we measure it when we use it. Therefore, each one of us makes a difference to our world.

Others aren't enough—*you* are needed! Your saltiness changes the flavor of the world.

It's the same with light. One more lighted candle decreases the darkness. You are significant!

In Roman times, soldiers were paid in salt; hence the question, "Are you worth your salt?" This is God's question to you this week. Are you what you ought to be?

Today I want you to compare Matthew 5:13 with two other cross references on salt. Under each reference list everything you learn about salt from that passage.

 MATTHEW 5:13

"You are the salt of the earth; but if the salt has become tasteless, how will it be made salty again? It is good for nothing anymore, except to be thrown out and trampled under foot by men."

 MARK 9:50

"Salt is good; but if the salt becomes unsalty, with what will you make it salty again? Have salt in yourselves, and be at peace with one another."

 LUKE 14:33–35

"So therefore, no one of you can be My disciple who does not give up all his own possessions. Therefore, salt is good; but if even salt has become tasteless, with what will it be seasoned? It is useless either for the soil or for the manure pile; it is thrown out. He who has ears to hear, let him hear."

Write in your own words what you think Jesus is saying in Matthew 5:13. How would you explain this passage to another person in the light of what you have learned from Mark 9:50 and Luke 14:33-35?

— D A Y   T W O —

The Word of God is a timeless book. It speaks to men and women of all generations.

At the same time, however, its contents were penned within a context of particular times, cultures, and histories. When interpreting Scripture, it must always be considered within the framework of these contexts.

The salt of biblical times was not like our pure, refined salt. Instead, it was found in varying degrees of purity. Its uses were as varied as its degrees of purity.

In Leviticus, God instructs His people to use salt in their sacrifices. A covenant of salt is referred to in the Old Testament. Lot's wife was turned into a pillar of salt.

As in our time, salt was used to season food, to make it more palatable. The apostle Paul had this use in mind when he wrote to the believers at Colossae: "Let your speech always be with grace, seasoned, as it were, with salt, so that you may know how you should respond to each person" (Colossians 4:6).

Salt was used then, as it still is, as a preservative, to stop the spread of corruption, and as an antiseptic to kill germs. Inferior sorts of salt were used to decompose the soil or as a fertilizer. Too much salt in the soil, however, would result in the sterility of the earth so that nothing could grow. A conquering nation might sow a city with salt, demonstrating the city's irretrievable ruin (see Judges 9:45). Finally, when salt had no savor at all and was simply a crystal of some sort, it was cast out on the ground or used to make paths for men to tread upon.

In light of the historical context, it becomes easier to understand the passages from the gospels that you studied yesterday, doesn't it? Luke 14:35 summarizes part of what we have seen: "It is useless either for the soil or for the manure pile; it is thrown out."

Apparently the salt that Jesus referred to was of a different composition than our salt. It could lose its savor altogether and become totally useless.

Jesus is talking about the character of a Christian. The Christian's life is to have a distinctive *flavor*. If it loses this character, it is worthless. If you and I are not what we ought to be, then we really have no worth as far as this earth is concerned.

It's the same way with the related metaphor, "You are the light of the world." Light has an obvious character. It is to be seen of men. The purpose of a lamp or a candle is to give light. If it doesn't give light, *what good is it?* It has no purpose or value.

When I think of salt and light, I cannot help but think also of the vine and branches mentioned in John 15:1-6. A branch is good for one thing—bearing fruit. If a branch does not bear fruit, it is thrown away and dries up. Men gather such branches and use them as fuel for fires. There's nothing else that can be done with them.

A branch has a function.

Salt has a function.

Light has a function.

But fruitless branches, savorless salt, and lightless lamps have no function at all!

In essence, Paul is saying the same thing in 1 Corinthians 9:27: "But I buffet my body and make it my slave, lest possibly, after I have preached to others, I myself should be disqualified."

The apostle is saying, "Listen, if my *body,* rather than God's Spirit, is going to dominate me, then God's going to have to disqualify me. I'm out of the running, out of the race. Why? Because I am not what I ought to be as a child of God. I have lost my true use and value."

In each of these word pictures, the message is essentially the same. The Christian life is not just a matter of doing, it's a matter of being. It's a matter of living out a God-ordained life, fulfilling God's ordained functions. If you neglect or refuse to do this, then you have no value to the kingdom of God. You are good for nothing.

Perhaps you would reply, "Wow, Kay, that's kind of tough. That's kind of hard teaching, isn't it? It seems pretty narrow."

Yes, it is. And a lot of people don't like that. They won't buy it. They want an easy believism, a gospel that makes no demands and doesn't call for a wholehearted commitment. They want to short-circuit the radical implications of a life of discipleship. They want their own "lite" brand of Christianity.

But you see, Beloved, we're not the ones who are calling the shots! God is. And like it or not, in statement after statement in the Sermon on the Mount, our Lord shows us just how small that gate into the kingdom really is and how narrow is the road leading to eternal life. Is it any wonder that few find it?

Are you salty salt? Does your presence in the world cause others to thirst after the Fountain of Living Water? Is your life such that it hinders the spread of corruption in your society, in your city, in your schools? Why don't you spend some time with God in prayer now?

In honest objectivity ask Him to show you how salty you really are.

— DAY   THREE —

The first mention of salt in the Bible is strange and shocking.

Here is what it says in Genesis 19:26: "But [Lot's] wife, from behind him, looked back; and she became a pillar of salt."

God planned to rain fire and brimstone on Sodom and Gomorrah, two evil cities in the plain of the Jordan. But before He could do that, He had to remove Lot (Abraham's nephew) and Lot's family out of the doomed city. But as they left Sodom, Lot's wife ignored the angel's warnings and stopped to look back. Her decision cost her life. She became a pillar of salt where she stood.

But there is another "salt connection" in this story. In essence, Lot lost his salt in Sodom!

Lot had a problem. His focus was wrong.

When you follow Lot's story through the pages of Genesis, you see a string of self centered, inevitably tragic choices. It begins in Genesis 13. Because of the strife between the herdsmen of Lot and those of Abraham, Abraham offers Lot the choice of a land that God had given to Abraham.

> And Lot lifted up his eyes and saw all the valley of the Jordan, that it was well watered everywhere—this was before the LORD destroyed Sodom and Gomorrah—like the garden of the LORD, like the land of Egypt as you go to Zoar. So Lot chose for himself all the valley of the Jordan. (Genesis 13:10-11)

Without consideration for his uncle, Lot chose the best for himself.

Next we find him pitching his tents toward Sodom, a city where "the men…were wicked exceedingly and sinners against the LORD" (Genesis 13:13). Just one chapter later, in Genesis 14:12, Lot is actually *living* in Sodom. And then in Genesis 19:1, we find him sitting in the gate of Sodom, the place where men of prominence in the city usually sat.

Stop now and read Genesis 19:1-17, printed below. Then answer the questions which follow.

❯ GENESIS 19:1-17

1 Now the two angels came to Sodom in the evening as Lot was sitting in the gate of Sodom. When Lot saw them, he rose to meet them and bowed down with his face to the ground.

2 And he said, "Now behold, my lords, please turn aside into your servant's house, and spend the night, and wash your feet; then you may rise early and go on your way." They said however, "No, but we shall spend the night in the square."

3 Yet he urged them strongly, so they turned aside to him and entered his house; and he prepared a feast for them, and baked unleavened bread, and they ate.

4 Before they lay down, the men of the city, the men of Sodom, surrounded the house, both young and old, all the people from every quarter;

5 and they called to Lot and said to him, "Where are the men who came to you tonight? Bring them out to us that we may have relations with them."

6 But Lot went out to them at the doorway, and shut the door behind him,

7 and said, "Please, my brothers, do not act wickedly.

8 "Now behold, I have two daughters who have not had relations with man; please let me bring them out to you, and do to them whatever you like; only do nothing to these men, inasmuch as they have come under the shelter of my roof."

9 But they said, "Stand aside." Furthermore, they said, "This one came in as an alien, and already he is acting like a judge; now we will treat you worse than them." So they pressed hard against Lot and came near to break the door.

10 But the men reached out their hands and brought Lot into the house with them, and shut the door.

11 And they struck the men who were at the doorway of the house with blindness, both small and great, so that they wearied themselves trying to find the doorway.

12 Then the men said to Lot, "Whom else have you here? A son-in-law, and your sons, and your daughters, and whomever you have in the city, bring them out of the place;

13 for we are about to destroy this place, because their outcry has become so great before the LORD that the LORD has sent us to destroy it."

14 And Lot went out and spoke to his sons-in-law, who were to marry his daughters, and said, "Up, get out of this place, for the LORD will destroy the city." But he appeared to his sons-in-law to be jesting.

15 And when morning dawned, the angels urged Lot, saying, "Up, take your wife and your daughters, who are here, lest you be swept away in the punishment of the city."

16 But he hesitated. So the men seized his hand and the hand of his wife and the hands of his daughters, for the compassion of the LORD was upon him; and they brought him out, and put him outside the city.

17 And it came about when they had brought them outside, that one said, "Escape for your life! Do not look behind you, and do not stay anywhere in the valley; escape to the mountains, lest you be swept away."

1. What did the men of Sodom want to do to the two angels who came as men to Lot's house?

2. When Lot rebuked the men, how did they respond to him (Genesis 19:9)? What does this tell you about his apparent relationship with them?

3. According to verse 14, what kind of influence did Lot have upon his sons-in-law?

Before we summarize, it is important for you to read 2 Peter 2:4-9, printed out for you on the next page. Answer the questions that follow, and then we will put it all together.

▶ 2 PETER 2:4-9

4 For if God did not spare angels when they sinned, but cast them into hell and committed them to pits of darkness, reserved for judgment;

5 and did not spare the ancient world, but preserved Noah, a preacher of righteousness, with seven others, when He brought a flood upon the world of the ungodly;

6 and if He condemned the cities of Sodom and Gomorrah to destruction by reducing them to ashes, having made them an example to those who would live ungodly thereafter;

7 and if He rescued righteous Lot, oppressed by the sensual conduct of unprincipled men

8 (for by what he saw and heard that righteous man, while living among them, felt his righteous soul tormented day after day with their lawless deeds),

9 then the Lord knows how to rescue the godly from temptation, and to keep the unrighteous under punishment for the day of judgment.

1. Why did God condemn the cities of Sodom and Gomorrah?

2. How does God refer to Noah in this passage?

3. How does He refer to Lot?

4. Was Lot comfortable living in Sodom? As you answer this question, make sure you refer to 2 Peter 2:4-9 to support your answer.

From 2 Peter 2 we see that Lot believed God and was apparently considered righteous by God, for God could not destroy Sodom until Lot left the city.

He was righteous…but it seems he had lost his salt.

Lot lived in Sodom but refused to partake in the city's evil deeds. Yet what kind of an impact did he have upon Sodom? Why was he living there? How had he obtained a position of respectability? Apparently by compromising and keeping his mouth shut! His life did not have a righteous impact upon those with whom he lived! His term "brother" appears to denote a tolerance and acceptance of these evil men.

Genesis 19:9 seems to imply that until this time Lot had neither opposed his neighbors nor called them to accountability for their actions. Lot's words to his sons-in-law apparently carried very little weight. When he tried to warn them of the approaching judgment, they thought it was a joke!

In Ephesians 5:11 the Lord tells us through Paul, "And do not participate in the unfruitful deeds of darkness, but instead even expose them." Not only had Lot failed to be "salty salt," he had also hidden God's light of truth under a basket. Although he did not participate in the unfruitful deeds of darkness, he apparently did not expose them! How can you sit at the gate and be a popular man when you expose the sins of those with whom you live? The two cannot possibly go together.

Lot was saved, but he had no witness among those with whom he lived, no effect upon his society, and very little influence with his own family. He had lost his salt. His life did not create a thirst for God among his neighbors.

Why is there so much corruption around us, Beloved? Is it because we have failed to be the salt of the earth? Statistics show that multiple millions of American Christians have not even registered to vote! Is that being salty salt?

When vile movies or places of obscene entertainment come to your town, do you sit in apathy in your salt shaker? Or do you get out into the world to stop the spread of corruption? Do you, as Ephesians 5 says, expose the unfruitful deeds of darkness? Do you stand firm against all the attacks of the enemy, Satan, or are you ignorant of his methods and devices? Do you keep abreast of current legislation and how to oppose bills that are in direct opposition to the principles and precepts of God's Word? Or do you sit in your salt shaker, criticizing those who are the salt of the earth? How I pray that God will speak to you in a very clear way so that your life will not be worthless, cast out, and trodden under foot of men in mockery.

George Truett once said, "You are either being corrupted by the world or you are salting it." There is no middle ground.

— D A Y   F O U R —

"Unbelievers are often kept from evil deeds," says the *Wycliffe Bible Commentary*, "because of a moral consciousness traceable to Christian influence."

If this is true, what does it tell you about Christian influence in the United States of America?

In our last two days of this study, we will look specifically at Jesus' statement, "You are the light of the world." As we said before, light has one purpose: to dispel darkness. In Matthew 5:16 Jesus' admonition is very clear. We are to let our light shine before men so that they may see our good works and glorify our Father in heaven.

Our good works cause the light to shine. But those good works are to be done in such a way that they do not glorify us but our Father. If they do not point men beyond us to the Father, then something is wrong with the way we are letting our lights shine.

I'm not saying that it's wrong for people to love you and appreciate you. This is obviously going to happen if you are used of God in a significant way in somebody's life. That love and appreciation, however, *should never stop with you.* It should rather bring the focus around the true Light, the Source of all Light, Jesus Christ. The lampstand is not significant, but the light that comes from the lampstand is. The lampstand is merely a vessel to bring light to those who are in its presence. Just as the moon reflects the sun's light, so we are to reflect the Son's light!

Let's look at some scriptures that will give us insight into the Light of the world and how we relate to that Light. Please read the following passage very carefully. Mark every reference to *light.*

❯ JOHN 1:1-9,14-17

1 In the beginning was the Word, and the Word was with God, and the Word was God.

2 He was in the beginning with God.

3 All things came into being by Him, and apart from Him nothing came into being that has come into being.

4 In Him was life, and the life was the light of men.

5 And the light shines in the darkness, and the darkness did not comprehend it.

⁶ There came a man, sent from God, whose name was John.

⁷ He came for a witness, that he might bear witness of the light, that all might believe through him.

⁸ He was not the light, but *came* that he might bear witness of the light.

⁹ There was the true light which, coming into the world, enlightens every man....

¹⁴ And the Word became flesh, and dwelt among us, and we beheld His glory, glory as of the only begotten from the Father, full of grace and truth.

¹⁵ John bore witness of Him, and cried out, saying, "This was He of whom I said, 'He who comes after me has a higher rank than I, for He existed before me.'"

¹⁶ For of His fulness we have all received, and grace upon grace.

¹⁷ For the Law was given through Moses; grace and truth were realized through Jesus Christ.

1. John 1:1 talks about the Word. John 1:14-17 tells us who the Word is. Who is it? What is His name?

2. According to John 1:4, what relationship did "this One" (the One of John 1:14-17) have to light? (Note: Before you answer, check John 1:9.)

3. What was John's relationship to the Light?

4. What do you think John 1:5 is saying?

 JOHN 8:12

Again therefore Jesus spoke to them, saying, "I am the light of the world; he who follows Me shall not walk in the darkness, but shall have the light of life."

What do you learn from this verse about those who follow Him?

 JOHN 9:5

"While I am in the world, I am the light of the world."

Jesus is no longer "in the world" as He was when He walked its pathways as a man among men. According to what you have studied this week, is there any light in the world now that Jesus has left? If so, describe that light.

Read the following passage, printed out below. (I love it!)

◗ J O H N   1 2 : 4 6

"I have come as light into the world, that everyone who believes in Me may not remain in darkness."

According to this verse what happens to those who really believe in Jesus?

Now let's summarize some of the things we have seen. Before He came into the world, Jesus was the Word of God, He was with God, and He was God. He always has been God, and He always will be God. In John 1:4 we saw that Jesus was the Source of light and He became the Light of men, which lifted humanity out of darkness, according to John 12:46.

As John was a witness of the Light so that people might believe through Him, so you and I are to be witnesses of the Light. Jesus, the Light of the world, has returned to the Father. Yet He has not left the world in darkness because we, His people, remain here.

As Matthew 5 says, you and I are the light of the world. But did He leave us on earth to hide our lights "under a peck-measure"? Of course not! The purpose of light is to be seen. "A city set on a hill cannot be hidden" (verse 14).

If you are a child of God, you are a part of that Holy City, the new Jerusalem, which will someday come down out of heaven from God. That city will have no need of the sun or moon to shine upon it, for the glory of God will illumine it. Its lamp will be the Lamb, and the nations will walk by His light (Revelation 21:2,23-24). Until that glorious day, you and I, who are citizens of heaven, are to be like a city set on a hill that cannot be hidden. We are to let those who grope and stumble in the darkness know where the true Light may be found.

This is why the apostle John is so adamant in his first letter.

And this is the message we have heard from Him and announce to you, that God is light, and in Him there is no darkness at all. If we say that we have fellowship with Him and yet walk in the darkness, we lie and do not practice the truth; but if we walk in the light as He Himself is in the light, we have fellowship with one another, and the blood of Jesus His Son cleanses us from all sin. (1 John 1:5-7)

You cannot walk in darkness and continue to claim a share in the Great Light, the Lord Jesus Christ. Fellowship is sharing something in common. If you say you have fellowship with Jesus and you are walking in darkness, you can know that you are lying because in Jesus there is no darkness. John tells us, "the one who says he abides in Him ought himself to walk in the same manner as He walked" (1 John 2:6).

Do you realize how many people say that they know God, that they belong to Him, and yet walk in darkness? Their very deeds, their entire lifestyles deny the reality of the light of God. Light dispels darkness. It never contributes to it! The two are totally incompatible.

Read the passage that follows, note the contrasts, and mark every reference to light and to darkness.

● 1 JOHN 2:9-11

9 The one who says he is in the light and yet hates his brother is in the darkness until now.

10 The one who loves his brother abides in the light and there is no cause for stumbling in him.

11 But the one who hates his brother is in the darkness and walks in the

darkness, and does not know where he is going because the darkness has blinded his eyes.

Now record what you observe from these verses:

THOSE IN THE LIGHT   THOSE IN DARKNESS

Those who truly have the life of God within them, who truly walk in the light, cannot walk in hatred. They must walk in love. Why? Because God is not only light, but also love (1 John 4:8).

Take time today, Beloved, to go to the Lord in prayer and ask Him if you are walking in the light. Ask Him to show you how your good works are glorifying His name so that you might be encouraged. Ask Him also to show you what good works you might do in order to glorify Him even more. Write down your insights.

– D A Y   F I V E –

If you are going to let your light shine before men so they may see your good works and glorify your Father in heaven, how are you going to walk?

Ephesians 5:1-16 has some very good insights for us regarding this matter. Take a few minutes and read that passage. Mark every reference to light as you have done in previous passages. Then I will give you some additional exercises to help you see more clearly what Paul is saying to us.

◗ EPHESIANS 5:1-16

1 Therefore be imitators of God, as beloved children;

2 and walk in love, just as Christ also loved you, and gave Himself up for us, an offering and a sacrifice to God as a fragrant aroma.

3 But do not let immorality or any impurity or greed even be named among you, as is proper among saints;

4 and there must be no filthiness and silly talk, or coarse jesting, which are not fitting, but rather giving of thanks.

5 For this you know with certainty, that no immoral or impure person or covetous man, who is an idolater, has an inheritance in the kingdom of Christ and God.

6 Let no one deceive you with empty words, for because of these things the wrath of God comes upon the sons of disobedience.

7 Therefore do not be partakers with them;

8 for you were formerly darkness, but now you are light in the Lord; walk as children of light

9 (for the fruit of the light consists in all goodness and righteousness and truth),

10 trying to learn what is pleasing to the Lord.

11 And do not participate in the unfruitful deeds of darkness, but instead even expose them;

12 for it is disgraceful even to speak of the things which are done by them in secret.

13 But all things become visible when they are exposed by the light, for everything that becomes visible is light.

14 For this reason it says,

"Awake, sleeper,

And arise from the dead,

And Christ will shine on you."

15 Therefore be careful how you walk, not as unwise men, but as wise,

16 making the most of your time, because the days are evil.

1. One of the key words in this passage is *walk*. In the preceding passage, mark each occurrence of the word *walk* and then make a list of everything you learn about how we are to walk.

2. Now read through the verses again and note everything we are to do if we walk as children of the light.

3. What is the most significant thing you have learned today? How has God spoken to you this week? What steps are you going to take in order to apply to your own life what He has said?

A number of years ago Jim Bird, our international director, was approached by Barry, one of his Precept students who had recently come to know Jesus Christ. Barry's life was being transformed through his diligent study of God's Word. But he was troubled.

Before he became a Christian, Barry had bought some stolen railroad ties. They had been taken from one railroad company and from a woman who owned a landscaping business. He knew when he purchased them that they were stolen, but it was such a good deal! (Or so he had thought at the time.)

As Barry studied the Sermon on the Mount, the Lord kept bringing those railroad ties to mind. The more he studied and the more he prayed, the more it troubled him. His homework on "mourning over sin" brought before him the issue of restitution. Finally he went to Jim for counsel.

Jim led Barry through the Scriptures for his answer.

And Barry chose to walk in obedience to what he had learned.

First, he went to the railroad company, hoping to confess his wrong to a clerk. No such clerk was available, but the receptionist told Barry that the "big boss" was available. So Barry swallowed hard and went into the man's office. He frankly confessed what he had done and told the railroad executive that he wanted to make restitution. Did they want the ties back? What could he do?

Barry's light was shining! The "big boss" saw it. The landscape lady saw it, too, when Barry confessed to her. When Jim told the story to my husband and me, we saw the light shining too. And now here you are, years and years later, reading Barry's story. You, too, can see the light! How our Father has been glorified through this young man's courageous actions! Barry was formerly walking in darkness, but after he met Jesus Christ and began walking in obedience to Him, he was walking as a child of light, dispelling the darkness.

O Beloved, as we conclude these brief weeks together in God's Word, remember that you are the salt of the earth. You are the light of the world. And the world sees the difference as you…

> walk in poverty of spirit,
>
> mourn over sin,
>
> bow in submission before His sovereignty,
>
> walk in true meekness before God and man,
>
> hunger and thirst for righteousness,
>
> and count it all joy when you are persecuted for righteousness.

Your life will truly reflect Him. Your salt will keep its savor and do its work. Your light will help dispel the darkness that threatens to cover your corner of the world. So seek Him with all your heart, soul, mind, and strength. In His love and by His power, you and I can light up this dark, despairing world!

MEMORY VERSE

You are the salt of the earth; but if the salt has become tasteless, how will it be made salty again? It is good for nothing anymore, except to be thrown out and trampled under foot by men. You are the light of the world. A city set on a hill cannot be hidden.… Let your light shine before men in such a way that they may see your good works, and glorify your Father who is in heaven.

MATTHEW 5:13-14,16

SMALL-GROUP DISCUSSION QUESTIONS

1. Have the class quote the memory verse for the week.
2. Why did Jesus use the metaphors of salt and light to describe a Christian?
3. Discuss the varied uses of salt in biblical days.
4. What did you learn about salt that relates to our lives as children of God?
5. Can you see some ways that you act as salt? Could you be saltier? Have you lost your savor?
6. Discuss what you learned about Lot. What was his ambition? His situation? What was Lot's impact on his society?
7. Compare Lot's life to your own. In what ways have you failed to impact your society? Why?
8. What did you learn about light and the Christian's relationship to it?
9. What is the message of John 5:5-7? How does it compare with John 8:12; 9:5; 12:46? Read theses passages and discuss them.
10. What about those who claim to know Christ but walk in darkness as a habit of life? What does the Word of God say? Where?
11. Talk about specific ways in which our light shines.

12. What has happened in your life in these past weeks? What has changed? How? What do you want to happen?
13. Have the class close by praying for one another. Then discuss the benefits of finishing the study of the Sermon on the Mount by doing *Lord, I'm Torn Between Two Masters.*

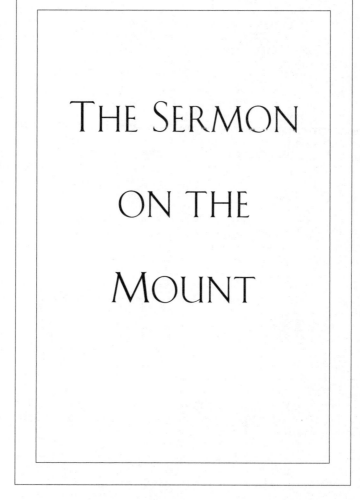

THE SERMON

ON THE

MOUNT

CHAPTER 5

¹ And when He saw the multitudes, He went up on the mountain; and after He sat down, His disciples came to Him.

² And opening His mouth He began to teach them, saying,

³ "Blessed are the poor in spirit, for theirs is the kingdom of heaven.

⁴ "Blessed are those who mourn, for they shall be comforted.

⁵ "Blessed are the gentle, for they shall inherit the earth.

⁶ "Blessed are those who hunger and thirst for righteousness, for they shall be satisfied.

⁷ "Blessed are the merciful, for they shall receive mercy.

⁸ "Blessed are the pure in heart, for they shall see God.

⁹ "Blessed are the peacemakers, for they shall be called sons of God.

¹⁰ "Blessed are those who have been persecuted for the sake of righteousness, for theirs is the kingdom of heaven.

¹¹ "Blessed are you when men cast insults at you, and persecute you, and say all kinds of evil against you falsely, on account of Me.

¹² "Rejoice, and be glad, for your reward in heaven is great, for so they persecuted the prophets who were before you.

¹³ "You are the salt of the earth; but if the salt has become tasteless, how will it be made salty again? It is good for nothing anymore, except to be thrown out and trampled under foot by men.

¹⁴ "You are the light of the world. A city set on a hill cannot be hidden.

¹⁵ "Nor do men light a lamp, and put it under the peck-measure, but on the lampstand; and it gives light to all who are in the house.

¹⁶ "Let your light shine before men in such a way that they may see your good works, and glorify your Father who is in heaven.

¹⁷ "Do not think that I came to abolish the Law or the Prophets; I did not come to abolish, but to fulfill.

18 "For truly I say to you, until heaven and earth pass away, not the smallest letter or stroke shall pass away from the Law, until all is accomplished.

19 "Whoever then annuls one of the least of these commandments, and so teaches others, shall be called least in the kingdom of heaven; but whoever keeps and teaches them, he shall be called great in the kingdom of heaven.

20 "For I say to you, that unless your righteousness surpasses that of the scribes and Pharisees, you shall not enter the kingdom of heaven.

21 "You have heard that the ancients were told, 'YOU SHALL NOT COMMIT MURDER' and 'Whoever commits murder shall be liable to the court.'

22 "But I say to you that everyone who is angry with his brother shall be guilty before the court; and whoever shall say to his brother, 'Raca,' shall be guilty before the supreme court; and whoever shall say, 'You fool,' shall be guilty enough to go into the fiery hell.

23 "If therefore you are presenting your offering at the altar, and there remember that your brother has something against you,

24 leave your offering there before the altar, and go your way; first be reconciled to your brother, and then come and present your offering.

25 "Make friends quickly with your opponent at law while you are with him on the way, in order that your opponent may not deliver you to the judge, and the judge to the officer, and you be thrown into prison.

26 "Truly I say to you, you shall not come out of there, until you have paid up the last cent.

27 "You have heard that it was said, 'YOU SHALL NOT COMMIT ADULTERY';

28 but I say to you, that everyone who looks on a woman to lust for her has committed adultery with her already in his heart.

29 "And if your right eye makes you stumble, tear it out, and throw it from you; for it is better for you that one of the parts of your body perish, than for your whole body to be thrown into hell.

30 "And if your right hand makes you stumble, cut it off, and throw it from you; for it is better for you that one of the parts of your body perish, than for your whole body to go into hell.

31 "And it was said, 'WHOEVER DIVORCES HIS WIFE, LET HIM GIVE HER A CERTIFICATE OF DISMISSAL';

32 but I say to you that everyone who divorces his wife, except for the cause of unchastity, makes her commit adultery; and whoever marries a divorced woman commits adultery.

33 "Again, you have heard that the ancients were told, 'YOU SHALL NOT MAKE FALSE VOWS, BUT SHALL FULFILL YOUR VOWS TO THE LORD.'

34 "But I say to you, make no oath at all, either by heaven, for it is the throne of God,

35 or by the earth, for it is the footstool of His feet, or by Jerusalem, for it is THE CITY OF THE GREAT KING.

36 "Nor shall you make an oath by your head, for you cannot make one hair white or black.

37 "But let your statement be, 'Yes, yes' or 'No, no'; and anything beyond these is of evil.

38 "You have heard that it was said, 'AN EYE FOR AN EYE, AND A TOOTH FOR A TOOTH.'

39 "But I say to you, do not resist him who is evil; but whoever slaps you on your right cheek, turn to him the other also.

40 "And if anyone wants to sue you, and take your shirt, let him have your coat also.

41 "And whoever shall force you to go one mile, go with him two.

42 "Give to him who asks of you, and do not turn away from him who wants to borrow from you.

43 "You have heard that it was said, 'YOU SHALL LOVE YOUR NEIGHBOR, and hate your enemy.'

44 "But I say to you, love your enemies, and pray for those who persecute you

45 in order that you may be sons of your Father who is in heaven; for He causes His sun to rise on the evil and the good, and sends rain on the righteous and the unrighteous.

46 "For if you love those who love you, what reward have you? Do not even the tax-gatherers do the same?

47 "And if you greet your brothers only, what do you do more than others? Do not even the Gentiles do the same?

48 "Therefore you are to be perfect, as your heavenly Father is perfect.

CHAPTER 6

1 "Beware of practicing your righteousness before men to be noticed by them; otherwise you have no reward with your Father who is in heaven.

2 "When therefore you give alms, do not sound a trumpet before you, as the hypocrites do in the synagogues and in the streets, that they may be honored by men. Truly I say to you, they have their reward in full.

3 "But when you give alms, do not let your left hand know what your right hand is doing

4 that your alms may be in secret; and your Father who sees in secret will repay you.

5 "And when you pray, you are not to be as the hypocrites; for they love to stand and pray in the synagogues and on the street corners, in order to be seen by men. Truly I say to you, they have their reward in full.

6 "But you, when you pray, go into your inner room, and when you have shut your door, pray to your Father who is in secret, and your Father who sees in secret will repay you.

7 "And when you are praying, do not use meaningless repetition, as the Gentiles do, for they suppose that they will be heard for their many words.

8 "Therefore do not be like them; for your Father knows what you need, before you ask Him.

9 "Pray, then, in this way:

'Our Father who art in heaven,

Hallowed be Thy name.

10 'Thy kingdom come.

Thy will be done,

On earth as it is in heaven.

11 'Give us this day our daily bread.

12 'And forgive us our debts, as we also have forgiven our debtors.

13 'And do not lead us into temptation, but deliver us from evil. [For Thine is the kingdom, and the power, and the glory, forever. Amen.]'

14 "For if you forgive men for their transgressions, your heavenly Father will also forgive you.

15 "But if you do not forgive men, then your Father will not forgive your transgressions.

16 "And whenever you fast, do not put on a gloomy face as the hypocrites do, for they neglect their appearance in order to be seen fasting by men. Truly I say to you, they have their reward in full.

17 "But you, when you fast, anoint your head, and wash your face

18 so that you may not be seen fasting by men, but by your Father who is in secret; and your Father who sees in secret will repay you.

19 "Do not lay up for yourselves treasures upon earth, where moth and rust destroy, and where thieves break in and steal.

20 "But lay up for yourselves treasures in heaven, where neither moth nor rust destroys, and where thieves do not break in or steal;

21 for where your treasure is, there will your heart be also.

22 "The lamp of the body is the eye; if therefore your eye is clear, your whole body will be full of light.

23 "But if your eye is bad, your whole body will be full of darkness. If therefore the light that is in you is darkness, how great is the darkness!

24 "No one can serve two masters; for either he will hate the one and love the other, or he will hold to one and despise the other. You cannot serve God and mammon.

25 "For this reason I say to you, do not be anxious for your life, as to what you shall eat, or what you shall drink; nor for your body, as to what you shall put on. Is not life more than food, and the body than clothing?

26 "Look at the birds of the air, that they do not sow, neither do they reap, nor gather into barns, and yet your heavenly Father feeds them. Are you not worth much more than they?

27 "And which of you by being anxious can add a single cubit to his life's span?

28 "And why are you anxious about clothing? Observe how the lilies of the field grow; they do not toil nor do they spin,

29 yet I say to you that even Solomon in all his glory did not clothe himself like one of these.

30 "But if God so arrays the grass of the field, which is alive today and tomorrow is thrown into the furnace, will He not much more do so for you, O men of little faith?

31 "Do not be anxious then, saying, 'What shall we eat?' or 'What shall we drink?' or 'With what shall we clothe ourselves?'

32 "For all these things the Gentiles eagerly seek; for your heavenly Father knows that you need all these things.

33 "But seek first His kingdom and His righteousness; and all these things shall be added to you.

34 "Therefore do not be anxious for tomorrow; for tomorrow will care for itself. Each day has enough trouble of its own.

CHAPTER 7

1 "Do not judge lest you be judged.

2 "For in the way you judge, you will be judged; and by your standard of measure, it will be measured to you.

3 "And why do you look at the speck that is in your brother's eye, but do not notice the log that is in your own eye?

4 "Or how can you say to your brother, 'Let me take the speck out of your eye,' and behold, the log is in your own eye?

5 "You hypocrite, first take the log out of your own eye, and then you will see clearly to take the speck out of your brother's eye.

6 "Do not give what is holy to dogs, and do not throw your pearls before swine, lest they trample them under their feet, and turn and tear you to pieces.

7 "Ask, and it shall be given to you; seek, and you shall find; knock, and it shall be opened to you.

8 "For everyone who asks receives, and he who seeks finds, and to him who knocks it shall be opened.

9 "Or what man is there among you, when his son shall ask him for a loaf, will give him a stone?

10 "Or if he shall ask for a fish, he will not give him a snake, will he?

11 "If you then, being evil, know how to give good gifts to your children, how much more shall your Father who is in heaven give what is good to those who ask Him!

12 "Therefore, however you want people to treat you, so treat them, for this is the Law and the Prophets.

13 "Enter by the narrow gate; for the gate is wide, and the way is broad that leads to destruction, and many are those who enter by it.

14 "For the gate is small, and the way is narrow that leads to life, and few are those who find it.

15 "Beware of the false prophets, who come to you in sheep's clothing, but inwardly are ravenous wolves.

16 "You will know them by their fruits. Grapes are not gathered from thorn bushes, nor figs from thistles, are they?

17 "Even so, every good tree bears good fruit; but the bad tree bears bad fruit.

18 "A good tree cannot produce bad fruit, nor can a bad tree produce good fruit.

19 "Every tree that does not bear good fruit is cut down and thrown into the fire.

20 "So then, you will know them by their fruits.

21 "Not everyone who says to Me, 'Lord, Lord,' will enter the kingdom of heaven; but he who does the will of My Father who is in heaven.

22 "Many will say to Me on that day, 'Lord, Lord, did we not prophesy in Your name, and in Your name cast out demons, and in Your name perform many miracles?'

23 "And then I will declare to them, 'I never knew you; DEPART FROM ME, YOU WHO PRACTICE LAWLESSNESS.'

24 "Therefore everyone who hears these words of Mine, and acts upon them, may be compared to a wise man, who built his house upon the rock.

25 "And the rain descended, and the floods came, and the winds blew, and burst against that house; and yet it did not fall, for it had been founded upon the rock.

26 "And everyone who hears these words of Mine, and does not act upon them, will be like a foolish man, who built his house upon the sand.

27 "And the rain descended, and the floods came, and the winds blew, and burst against that house; and it fell, and great was its fall."

28 The result was that when Jesus had finished these words, the multitudes were amazed at His teaching;

29 for He was teaching them as one having authority, and not as their scribes.

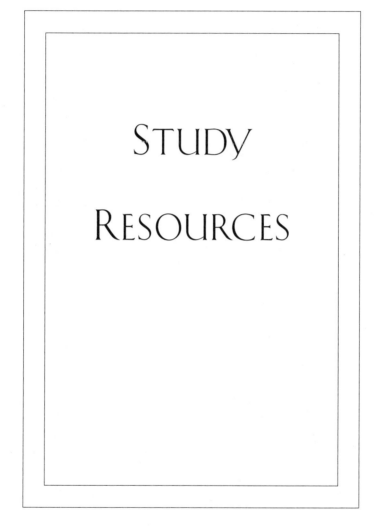

STUDY

RESOURCES

HOW TO MARK YOUR BIBLE

One of the things we at Precept Ministries International teach you to do in inductive Bible study is to find the key words in the passage you're studying and to mark them in a distinctive way. This is a very helpful and important element of the essential Bible study step known as observation—discovering exactly what the text says. So many times a Scripture passage is misinterpreted simply because the initial work of accurate observation has not been done. Remembering to mark key words will help you not to overlook this critical step.

WHAT ARE KEY WORDS?

Key words or phrases are those that are essential to the text. If they were to be removed, you would find it difficult or impossible to grasp the essence of what the passage is about. Like keys, these words "unlock" the meaning of the text. Recognizing them will help you uncover the author's intended purpose and emphasis in his message.

Key words can be nouns, descriptive words, or action words. Very often an author will repeat these words or phrases in order to emphasize his message. They may be repeated throughout an entire book—like the key words *love* and *abide,* which we see throughout the book of 1 John. Or they may be repeated throughout a shorter section of text, as with the key word *fellowship,* which is used four times in the first chapter of 1 John but not elsewhere in the book.

In the "Lord" series of Bible studies, you will often be asked to find and mark certain key words or phrases in the passage you're studying. This is a method that you will want to make a lifelong habit in your personal Bible study.

HOW TO MARK KEY WORDS

Marking key words can be done in several ways.

1. You can use different colors or a combination of colors to highlight

different words. When I mark a passage, I like to choose a color that to me best reflects the word I'm marking. I color references to God in yellow because God is light and in Him there is no darkness. I color sin brown. Any Old Testament reference to the temple is colored blue.

2. You can use a variety of symbols—simply drawing a circle around a word, underlining it, or marking it with a symbol of your own creation, such as these:

$$O \; \triangle \; \text{uuu} \; \mathcal{E}^{3}$$

When I use symbols, I try to devise one that best pictures the word. For example, the key words *repent* and *repentance* in Matthew 3 might be marked with the symbol ⟲ since in Scripture this word's root meaning represents a change of mind, which often leads to a change in direction.

3. You can combine colors with symbols. For example:

- In 1 John 3, the key word *love* could be marked with a red heart like this: ♡ If you want to distinguish God's love from man's, you could color God's heart yellow and man's red.
- Every reference to the devil or evil spirits could be marked with a red pitchfork. ⚔
- Every occurrence of covenant could be colored red and boxed in with yellow.

The *New Inductive Study Bible* (NISB) has a whole page of suggested markings for key words used throughout the Bible.

A WORD OF CAUTION

When looking for key words, sometimes the tendency is to mark too many words. For example, I rarely mark references to God and to Jesus Christ unless it is significant to understanding the message. For instance, the phrases "in Christ" and "in Him" are significant to understanding the message of Ephesians 1–3. If you marked every reference to Jesus in some of the gospel accounts, your Bible would be too marked up. So you need to use discretion. (I always mark every reference to the Holy Spirit because He is not referred to often, and there is much confusion about the person and ministry of the Holy Spirit.)

Remember to look for those words that relate to the foundational theme of the text. Sometimes a key word may not be repeated frequently, but you know it is key because without it you would not know the essence of what the author is talking about in that passage.

BE SURE TO MARK KEY-WORD SYNONYMS AND PRONOUNS

Synonyms for a key word would be marked the same way you mark the key word. For example, you would mark identically the word *devil* and the phrase "evil one" in Ephesians 6:10-18.

And be sure to mark pronouns (I, you, he, she, it, we, our, and so on) the same way you would mark the words to which they refer. In 1 Timothy 3:1-7, for example, you would mark the pronouns *he* and *his* in the same way you did the key word *overseer* in that passage.

For consistency, you may want to list on an index card the key symbols and colors you like using for certain words and keep that card in your Bible.

IMMEDIATE IDENTIFICATION

With a passage's key words marked in this way, you can look at the text and immediately spot the word's usage and importance. In the future you'll quickly be able to track key subjects and identify significant truths in any passage you've studied and marked.

CREATE LISTS FROM KEY WORDS

After you mark key words, you will find it helpful to list what you learn from the text by the use of the key word. For instance, once you mark the word *sin* in 1 John 3, you would make a list of what the text tells you about sin. As you look at each marked key word, list anything that would answer the questions *who, what, when, where, why,* or *how* about sin. You will be not only surprised but also delighted at the truths you can learn from this simple process of observation.

For more on how to mark your Bible and on the inductive Bible study approach, you may want to use the *New Inductive Study Bible* (from Harvest House Publishers), or you can reach us at Precept Ministries International by referring to the contact information in the back of this book.

GUIDELINES FOR GROUP USE

This study book, as well as all those in the "Lord" series, can be used for home Bible-study groups, Sunday-school classes, family devotions, and a great variety of other group situations. Here are some things to keep in mind as you use this study in a group setting to minister to others.

- Prayerfully commit the entire study to the Lord, seeking His direction for every step.

- As your group forms, encourage each member to purchase an individual copy of this book.

- For your first meeting you can show your students how to get started in their first lesson; work through a part of the lesson together so that they know what to do. Each student should then be able to complete on their own the study preparation for chapter 1 before the next class. (Encourage each student to do this faithfully week by week.)

- From the second meeting on, the weekly pattern should be to discuss first what you each have learned from your own study during the preceding week. Then, if you so desire, you could have a teacher present an in-depth message on the material just studied. Or you could listen to or watch the teaching available on CD or DVD for this series. Just make sure that the teaching CD or DVD follows the class discussion rather than precedes it. You want your group to have the joy of discovery and discussion.

- The group discussion questions following each chapter in this book are to aid you in leading a discussion of that week's material. However, merely having these questions will not be enough for a really lively and successful discussion. The better you know your material, the greater freedom you will have in leading. Therefore, Beloved, be faithful in your own study and remain dependent upon the ministry of the Holy Spirit, who is there to lead you and guide you into all truth and who will enable you to fulfill the good work God has foreordained for you. (As the group's leader, it would be ideal if you could either read the entire book first or do several weeks' study in advance, so you know where you're going and can grasp the scope of the material covered in this study.)

- Each week as you prepare to lead the group's discussion, pray and ask the Father what your particular group needs to learn and how you can best cover the material. Pray with pen in hand. Make a list of what the Lord shows you. Then create your own questions or select from the questions at the end of each chapter, which will help stimulate and guide the group members in the Lord's direction within the time you have.

- Remember that your group members will find the greatest sense of accomplishment in discussing what they've learned in their own study, so try to stick to the subject at hand in your discussion. This will keep the class from becoming frustrated. Make sure the answers and insights come from the Word of God and are always in accordance with the whole counsel of God.

- Strive in your group to create an atmosphere of love, safety, and caring. Be concerned about one another. Bear one another's burdens and so fulfill the law of Christ—the law of love (Galatians 6:2). We desperately need one another.

Please know that I thank our Father for you and your willingness to assume this critical role of establishing God's people in God's Word. I know that this process produces glory and reverence for Him. So press on, valiant one. He is coming, bringing in the kingdom in all its glory, and His reward is with Him to give to each one of us according to our deeds.

The "Lord" Series: An Overview

My burden—and calling—is to help Christians (or interested or desperate inquirers) see for themselves what the Word of God has to teach on significant and relevant life-related subjects. So many people are weak and unstable in their Christianity because they don't know truth for themselves; they only know what others have taught them. These books, therefore, are designed to involve you in the incomparably enriching experience of daily study in God's Word.

Each book has been thoroughly tested and has already had an impact on a multitude of lives. Let me introduce the full series to you.

Lord, I Want to Know You is a foundational study for the "Lord" books. In this seventeen-week study you'll discover how God's character is revealed through His names, such as Creator, Healer, Protector, Provider, and many more. Within the names of God you'll encounter strength for your worst trials, comfort for your heart's deepest pain, and provision for your soul's greatest need. As you come to know Him more fully—the power of His glorious name and the depth of His infinite love—your walk with God will be transformed and your faith will be increased.

Lord, Heal My Hurts is, understandably, one of the most popular studies in this series. If you're in touch with the world, you know that people around you are in great pain. We run to many sources for relief when we are in pain. Some of us turn to other people; many escape into drugs, work, further education, and even hobbies. But in God you can find salvation from any situation, from any hurt. In this thirteen-week study you'll see that, no matter what you've done or what's been done to you, God wants to become your refuge…He loves you and desires your wholeness…and He offers healing for your deepest wounds.

Lord, I Need Grace to Make It Today will reveal to you in fresh power the amazing truth that God's grace is available for *every* situation, no matter how difficult, no matter how terrible. You'll gain the confidence that God will use you for His glory, as His grace enables you to persevere regardless of your need, regardless of your circumstances, and despite the backward pull of your flesh. You will see and know that the Lord and His all-sufficient grace will always be with you. A highlight of this nine-week course is your study of the book of Galatians and its liberating message about our freedom in Christ.

Lord, I'm Torn Between Two Masters opens your understanding to the kind of life that is truly pleasing to God. If you've known discouragement because you felt you could never measure up to God's standards or if you've ever felt unbearably stretched by the clash of life's priorities, this nine-week study of the Sermon on the Mount will lead you into a new freedom that will truly clear your vision and fortify your heart. You'll be encouraged to entwine your thoughts, hopes, dreams, and desires around heavenly things, and you'll find your life transformed by choosing to seek first God's kingdom and His righteousness.

Lord, Only You Can Change Me is an nine-week devotional study on character that draws especially on the so-called Beatitudes of Matthew 5. If you've ever been frustrated at not being all you wanted to be for the Lord or at not being able to change, you'll find in this study of Christ's teaching the path to true inner transformation that is accomplished only through the work of the indwelling Holy Spirit. You will learn the achievable reality of a godly life and the fulfillment it can bring.

Lord, Where Are You When Bad Things Happen is a critically important study in preparing you for times of trial. In this ten-week course you'll be grounded in the knowledge and confidence of God's sovereignty as you study especially the book of Habakkuk and see how God works in and through difficult and demanding situations. More than that, you'll learn what it means to live by faith…and to rest the details of your life in His hands.

Lord, Is It Warfare? Teach Me to Stand is a study that trains you for spiritual battle. God's Word tells us that our adversary, the devil, goes about like a roaring lion seeking whom he may devour (1 Peter 5:8). Many times we either don't recognize this enemy, or we're scared by his roar. We would like him to go away, but it's not that simple. In this eleven-week study you'll learn how to recognize Satan's tactics and how to be set free from bondage. As you focus your study especially on the book of Ephesians, you'll discover how to build an unshakable faith that makes victory yours for the taking. (This is the most challenging of the "Lord" books and requires an average of two to two and a half hours of weekly preparation to complete the assignments.)

Lord, Give Me a Heart for You examines the anatomy of a heart for God—what it looks like, what it feels like, and how you can become a person whose sole passion is to please God. By walking you through the words of the apostle Paul in 2 Corinthians and Acts, as well as other portions of Scripture, this revolutionary eight-week study equips you to fight the good fight and keep the faith in the daily and difficult circumstances of life. Paul's vulnerability will touch your heart as you realize how much this great man of God is just like you in the battles and fears, conflicts and pressures of serving God in a world of opposition. Through this compelling study, you will learn how to tap God's power in your weakness, to look beyond the temporal to the eternal, and to be prepared for whatever life holds.

Beloved, I have written these books so that you can have insight from God's Word on the pertinent issues of life—not only for yourself, but also for your ministry to others.

Know that you are on my heart because you are precious to God and I long to see you live as more than a conqueror, fulfilling God's purpose for your life.

NOTES

CHAPTER TWO

1. Marvin R. Vincent, *Word Studies in the New Testament* (Grand Rapids: Eerdmans, 1976), 35.
2. D. A. Carson, *The Sermon on the Mount: An Evangelical Exposition of Matthew Five through Seven* (Grand Rapids: Baker, 1978), 118-119.
3. Carson, *The Sermon on the Mount*, 69, 118-119.

CHAPTER FOUR

1. W. E. Vine, *An Expository Dictionary of New Testament Words*, vol. 3 (Old Tappan: Revell, 1966), 56.
2. Lindley Baldwin, *Samuel Morris, The March of Faith* (Minneapolis: Dimension Books), 8.
3. Baldwin, *Samuel Morris*, 10-13.
4. Baldwin, *Samuel Morris*, 15-17.
5. Another excellent study that will take you much deeper in this area is *Lord, Where Are You When Bad Things Happen?*—a powerful study on the book of Habakkuk.

CHAPTER FIVE

1. Vine, *An Expository Dictionary*, 56.

CHAPTER SIX

1. Mrs. Howard Taylor, *Pastor Hsi* (London: OMF Books, 1949), 25.
2. Taylor, *Pastor Hsi*, 26.
3. Taylor, *Pastor Hsi*, 46-47, 50-52.
4. D. Martyn Lloyd-Jones, *Studies in the Sermon on the Mount* (Grand Rapids: Eerdmans, 1959), 73-74.

CHAPTER SEVEN

1. Vine, *An Expository Dictionary*, 62.
2. Vine, *An Expository Dictionary*, 60.
3. Vine, *An Expository Dictionary*, 207.

CHAPTER EIGHT

1. Don Richardson, *Peace Child* (Ventura: Gospel Light, 1976), 199-200.
2. Richardson, *Peace Child*, 201.
3. Haralan Popov, *Tortured for His Faith* (Grand Rapids: Zondervan, 1970), 126.
4. If you would like to pray for and write to those in prison for the gospel's sake, write the Reverend Georgi P. Vins, P.O. Box 1188, Elkhart, Indiana 46515-1188; ask for Prisoner Bulletin.

About Kay Arthur and Precept Ministries International

Kay Arthur, executive vice president and cofounder of Precept Ministries International, is known around the world as an inspiring Bible teacher, author, and conference speaker.

Kay and her husband, Jack, founded Precept Ministries in 1970 in Chattanooga, Tennessee. Started as a fledgling ministry for teens, Precept today is a worldwide outreach that establishes children, teens, and adults in God's Word, so that they can discover the Bible's truths for themselves. Precept inductive Bible studies are taught in all 50 states. The studies have been translated into nearly 70 languages, reaching almost 150 countries.

Kay is the author of more than 120 books and inductive Bible study courses, with a total of over 5 million books in print. Kay also hosts the national radio and television program *Precepts for Life*, which reaches a worldwide viewing audience of over 94 million.

Contact Precept Ministries for more information about inductive Bible studies in your area.

Precept Ministries International
P.O. Box 182218
Chattanooga, TN 37422-7218
800-763-8280
www.precept.org